SUCCESSFUL INDUCTION FOR NEW TEACHERS

9 Oct 2010

for Richard

SUCCESSFUL INDUCTION FOR NEW TEACHERS

A Guide for NQTs and Induction Tutors, Coordinators and Mentors

Sara Bubb

s.bubb@ioe.ac.uk

www.sarabubb.com

sara@

Los Angeles | London | New Delhi
Singapore | Washington DC

First published 2007

Reprinted 2009, 2010

SAGE Publications Ltd
1 Oliver's Yard
55 City Road
London EC1Y 1SP

SAGE Publications Inc
2455 Teller Road
Thousand Oaks, California 91320

SAGE Publications India Pvt Ltd
B 1/I 1 Mohan Cooperative Industrial Area
Mathura Road
New Delhi 110 044

SAGE Publications Asia-Pacific Pte Ltd
33 Pekin Street #02-01
Far East Square
Singapore 048763

Library of Congress Control Number: 2007932249

British Library Cataloguing in Publication Data

A catalogue record for this book is available from the British Library

ISBN 978-1-84787-033-9
ISBN 978-1-84787-034-6 (pbk)

Typeset by Pantek Arts Ltd, Maidstone, Kent
Printed in Great Britain by CPI Antony Rowe, Chippenham, Wiltshire
Printed on paper from sustainable resources

CONTENTS

${\sf A}$CKNOWLEDGEMENTS

I would like to thank all those who helped and contributed in some way to the writing of this book, particularly Kevan Bleach from Sneyd School in Walsall, Peter Earley from the Institute of Education, teachers in Lambeth, contributors to the NQT forum at the *Times Educational Supplement*, and all the teachers who come on my courses. They stimulate thought and help keep my feet on the ground! Most of all, thanks to Paul, Julian, Miranda and Oliver – for their proofreading, encouragement and understanding.

ABOUT THE AUTHOR

Sara Bubb is an experienced London teacher who helps staff in schools develop. She does this in many ways: through leading professional development, assessing, developing schemes, researching, and writing.

With a national and international reputation in the induction of new teachers and professional development, Sara speaks at conferences and runs courses throughout the country and abroad (e.g. Norway, Taiwan) on topics such as helping staff develop, observation skills, induction, developing pedagogical skills, leading continuing professional development (CPD), subject leadership, monitoring teaching and implementing performance management. She has featured on and been a consultant for eight Teachers TV programmes. She trains a broad range of people, including inspectors, assessors, advisers, consultants, Fasttrack, TeachFirst and advanced skills teachers.

Sara assesses advanced skills, excellent, overseas trained and graduate teachers and higher level teaching assistants and was an external assessor for Threshold. She has inspected over 25 primary schools.

As a senior lecturer at the Institute of Education (0.2) she works on PGCE and Masters programmes and set up the employment-based routes (OTT and GTP) to QTS. She is lead director of the CfBT Education Trust-funded Sef2Si – From Self Evaluation To School Improvement: The Importance Of Professional Development – project. She co-directed the DfES-funded national research Project on the Effectiveness of the Induction Year, was deputy director of the TDA systematic review of induction research and has helped the Northern Ireland GTC revise their teacher competences.

On a 0.2 secondment to the DCSF London Challenge team, Sara is the consultant for Chartered London Teacher status – a scheme involving over 38,600 teachers. She is the London Gifted & Talented Early Years network leader, working with staff in reception and nursery classes to enhance their provision for all children, especially the most able.

She has written books and numerous articles on induction, professional development, workload, and performance management. She is the new teacher expert at the *Times Educational Supplement*, and writes articles, a weekly advice column and answers questions on its website.

Abbreviations

AB	Appropriate body
AST	Advanced skills teacher
ATL	Association of Teachers and Lecturers
CEDP	Career entry and development profile
CLT	Chartered London Teacher
CPD	Continuing professional development
DCSF	Department for Children, Schools and Families
DfEE	Department for Education and Employment
DfES	Department for Education and Skills
GTC	General Teaching Council
GTCE	General Teaching Council for England
GTCS	General Teaching Council for Scotland
ICT	Information and communications technology
ISCTIP	Independent Schools Council Teacher Induction Panel
NASUWT	National Union of Schoolmasters Union of Women Teachers
NQT	Newly qualified teacher
NUT	National Union of Teachers
Ofsted	Office for Standards in Education
PGCE	Postgraduate certificate in education
PPA	Planning, preparation and assessment
QTS	Qualified teacher status
SEN	Special educational needs
SENCO	Special educational needs coordinator
SMT	Senior management team
TDA	Training and Development Agency for Schools
TES	*Times Educational Supplement*
TLA	Teacher Learning Academy
TSN	Teacher Support Network
TTA	Teacher Training Agency

INTRODUCTION

Since you're reading this book I probably don't need to convince you how important induction is. I am passionate about supporting all school staff so that children and young people get the best possible deal. Investing in people right at the start of their career is crucial because, no matter how good initial training is, the first year as a fully fledged teacher will be tough, as this teacher says:

> I've found this year bloody hard work, sometimes crushingly so, and think I would have collapsed under it if it wasn't for the support of my school. (NQT, Term 3)

Many people leave their training on a high having had a terrific teaching practice and expecting to build on that success. However, it's more realistic for people to prepare for turbulence rather than a smooth trip because of course the ride will be rocky: newly qualified teachers (NQTs) have to do exactly the same job as their more experienced colleagues. It really is crazy to throw new teachers into full responsibility for children's learning! Still, everyone in education needs to help them do the best that they can, and induction is there to do just that. It benefits not only NQTs but also those who support and assess them. And of course all the current and future pupils that new teachers work with will learn more and be happier. What better investment could we make?

However, individual new teachers' experience of induction is hugely variable. In the national evaluation of induction in 2000–02 (Totterdell *et al.*, 2002), we found that a fifth of NQTs did not get the 10 per cent reduced timetable they were entitled to; a fifth did not think their induction tutor gave useful advice; one in 11 hadn't observed any other teachers teaching despite having time to do so; three-quarters had some non-teaching responsibility; and half felt they taught classes with challenging behaviour. It's simply not fair. Although there are meant to be procedures for NQTs to air dissatisfaction at both school and local authority level, they're rarely used. Who's going to complain about their assessors?

Induction also needs to be done well because of the dire consequences of failing. You do know that people who fail induction are banned from teaching in maintained and non-maintained special schools for evermore, don't you? The failure rate is tiny – in the last three years 87 people have failed and 74,000 have passed induction. But are the 87 who are for ever banned from teaching in schools people who we'd all agree shouldn't teach? Perhaps they were just unlucky. And what about the others who jump before they're pushed? There are mysterious gaps in the figures because about 34,000 people get qualified teacher status (QTS) in England every year but only 25,000 pass induction.

So induction needs to be done well. Good teachers make good schools – but good schools also make good teachers. Where induction is successful:

- there are clear systems in place so that everyone knows how things work, who does what and when;

- the half-termly rhythm of induction is established;

- induction meetings have high status;

- strengths and needs are accurately diagnosed;

- support, including emotional support, comes from across the school and other NQTs;

- monitoring is not just through observation;

- observations are carried out well and relate to the standards, not inspection criteria;

- the reduced timetable is spent on a range of professional development activities to meet needs;

- new teachers seek and receive advice on managing workload;

- the whole school community is focused on learning – the children are learning and the adults are too, and people are interested in each other's development.

You're busy people with lots to do, so in this book I've tried to explain clearly, accessibly and concisely how to have a successful induction year. It's written both for new teachers themselves and those who support, monitor and assess them: headteachers, induction tutors, coordinators and mentors. I've used extracts from postings on the *Times Educational Supplement* (TES) new teacher staffroom to give a real feeling for the issues as well as some useful tips. Click on www.tes.co.uk/staffroom and see what friendly, entertaining and helpful people there are around.

The book starts with a chapter about looking after yourself, which is really important for new teachers and those who support them because teaching is stressful and there are few years harder than the first. I look at stages that new teachers might go through. It might be a comfort to know that if you're feeling low after the first six weeks you are perfectly normal and should hang on in there. Working with children in such large numbers and close proximity means lots of germs, so there are some tips about staying healthy. Forget about that interactive whiteboard, a teacher's voice is their most precious resource and it needs careful use and treatment, so there are some ideas about that too. I'm sure you're prepared for difficult children but are you ready for all the different adults that you have to work with in school? Most are marvellous but some can be thoughtless and downright rude, so I've included a section about staying strong and happy in the face of behaviour that might be less than professional – let's hope you don't need it.

With Chapter 2 we get into the induction regulations which, in spite of having been around around since 1999, still confuse people. I cover what induction is, what happens if you fail it and what new teachers are entitled to, as well as different models of completing induction and the roles and responsibilities of everyone involved. Chapter 3 explores the framework of teacher standards, focusing on the core ones that new teachers have to meet to complete induction. But I take a look at the standards that induction tutors and mentors will need to meet too.

There are three aspects to induction – support, monitoring and assessment – and the chapters that follow cover each of these. Chapter 4 explores key concepts in the support of teachers' development such as what professional development really means, how adults learn, the cycle of identifying, analysing and meeting needs and considering how to measure the impact of learning. There are some tips for keeping a professional portfolio and using the career entry and development profile (CEDP). This leads into Chapter 5 on analysing needs, setting objectives and drawing up action plans. Chapter 6 gives some ideas for the range of professional development activities that might meet new teachers' needs: coaching and mentoring, observing others, watching Teachers TV, learning through chatting, and going on courses and conferences. Being observed is a great way to develop as well as a way to monitor a new teacher's progress in the classroom, and Chapters 7 and 8 explore this. They are addressed to induction tutors and mentors rather than new teachers for obvious reasons – but new teachers should benefit from reading these chapters too. Discussing teaching both verbally and in writing is hard and something that induction tutors need to do with confidence, so Chapter 8 covers how to conduct a post-observation discussion and how to feed back judgements on teaching in writing.

The third component of induction is assessment, and this is the subject of Chapter 9. As well as some tips for reviewing progress at half term, there are pointers on getting the most out of the assessment meeting and on how the report should be written against the standards.

Chapter 10 is about moving on from the induction year, starting with using the questions for discussion in Transition Point 3 of the CEDP. It explains how teachers' pay and contracts are organised, before looking at how to make the most of performance management. At the back of the book there are some *pro formas* that might be useful for different aspects of induction – feel free to make them work for you.

I hope you enjoy reading this book and find it useful – induction helps everyone succeed.

Sara Bubb

July 2007, London

CHAPTER 1

Looking after yourself

- Stages you might go through

- Looking after yourself

- Your voice

- Managing your time

- Staying strong

- Coping with difficult people

- Keeping happy

Your first year in teaching will be rewarding and stimulating, but will undoubtedly be hard and very stressful. In this chapter I will look at ways to make it easier on a very practical level by explaining the stages you might go through; how to look after yourself and your voice in particular; how to manage your time and cope with difficult colleagues; and most importantly, how to keep happy.

Stages you might go through

There's a common perception that people should be able to teach well if they're qualified. Certainly, the pupils taught by a newly qualified teacher have as much right to a good education as those taught by someone with 20 years' experience. However, there's a huge difference between novice and experienced teachers. Like any skill or craft, learning to teach is a developmental process characterised by devastating disasters and spectacular successes. Teaching is a job that can never be done perfectly – one can always improve. Depressing, isn't it? Well, see teaching as acting: each lesson is a performance, and if one goes badly, the next can go better. Separate the performance from the real you. This will stop you feeling too wretched about lessons that don't go well. Remember that few people are natural-born teachers – everyone has to work at it and everyone can get better. The more you know about teaching and learning, the more you'll realise there is to know. That's what makes it such a great job!

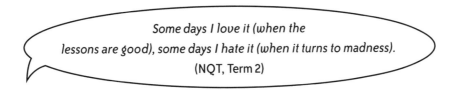

Some days I love it (when the lessons are good), some days I hate it (when it turns to madness).
(NQT, Term 2)

How you feel about teaching will probably change daily at first. One day will be great and leave you feeling positive and idealistic, but the next will be diabolical. As time goes by, good days will outnumber the bad ones, and you will realise that you are actually enjoying the job. There are recognised stages that teachers go through. Appreciating them will help keep you going and help you realise that you will need different levels and types of support at different times during your induction year. Figure 1.1 shows a trajectory of teachers' typical feelings during their first year. They start on a high in September but then reality strikes and they live from day to day, needing quick fixes and tips for survival. It's hard to solve problems because there are so many of them. Behaviour management is of particular concern, but they're too stressed and busy to reflect. Colds and sore throats seem permanent. Getting through all the Christmas activities is exhausting. In January, pupils return calmer and ready to work. Teachers can identify difficulties and think of solutions because there is some space in their life. Then they feel that they're mastering teaching, begin to enjoy it but don't want to tackle anything different or take on any radical new initiatives. Eventually, people will be ready for further challenges, want to try out different styles of teaching, new age groups, and take on more responsibilities.

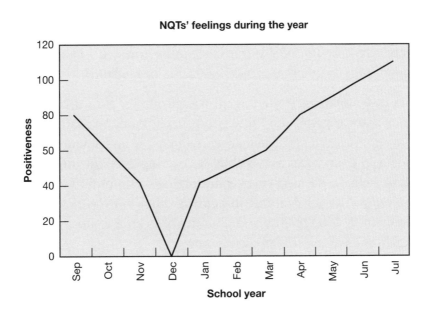

Figure 1.1 NQTs' feelings during the year (Bubb, 2005a, p.8)

Activity 1.1

Induction tutors: what can you do to help new teachers pace themselves?

Looking after yourself

Unless you're very lucky, illness will plague you during your first year of teaching like it has never done before. It won't be anything serious, I hope, but the rounds of sore throats, coughs and colds will leave you forgetting what it feels like to be well. Large numbers of children mean a lot of germs! When you're busy the easiest thing to do is to forget to look after yourself. Everyone knows that they function better with good nutrition and rest, but these seem to be the first things to be neglected.

Stress is defined as 'the adverse reaction people have to excessive pressures or other types of demand placed upon them. It arises when they worry they can't cope' (Health and Safety Executive, 2003). Stress affects different people in different ways, but you need to cope with its results and handle the causes. Given that there is no one cause of stress, there's no simple solution. Teaching is a stressful job and when you're new it's even worse, so you need to learn to manage stress. Look out for behaviour, mental health and physical symptoms. Are you getting irritable, tired, anxious, depressed, forgetful or accident-prone? Do you have aches and pains, headaches, digestive problems or seem to succumb to every germ that's doing the rounds? Are you eating more chocolate or drinking more? These are signals to you from your body that should not be ignored for long.

The first step is to recognise that the problem exists and tell someone how you feel – almost all teachers are kind and caring, but they can't help you unless they know what the problem is. The Teacher Support Network (TSN) has an excellent online stress assessment you can use to identify your levels of stress (www.teachersupport.info). I've done it and it seemed spot on. It gives you a report, and there's a facility for emailing it to anyone else who you think might benefit from knowing the result. It also contains suggestions for coping better. The Teacher Support Line is open every day and staffed by trained counsellors who can give support online (www.teachersupport.info) or by phone (08000 562 561 in England).

Analyse the causes of your stress. Try listing all your troubles, then dividing them into those over which you have some control, and those you haven't. Work on practical solutions to those over which you have some influence. There are certain people and situations that increase one's blood pressure, so avoid them as far as possible! Recovering from the 'high alert' positions that our bodies may have been in for long periods during the day is important, but hard to do. Do something that forces you to think about something other than work, something that needs your active involvement. A good quality and quantity of sleep is a must too. You need to be in tip-top form to teach, so invest in that body of yours.

Here are ten tips for looking after yourself:

1. Pace yourself. Don't over-commit yourself. You can't afford to burn out so plan some days to be less demanding.

2. Try to organise accommodation so that your journey is reasonable and that you feel comfortable when you get home.

3. Remember to eat well – don't skip meals. Snack on nutritious, high-energy foods such as bananas rather than chocolate bars. Get organised at weekends so that you have enough suitable food to last the week.

4. Take vitamin supplements. Vitamins and minerals will help your body fight off all the viruses that the pupils will bring into school.

5. Watch out for head lice – check your hair frequently with a very fine nit comb and take immediate action if you find any.

6. Monitor your caffeine and biscuit intake. Although they're the staple diet of many staffrooms, they really aren't much good for you.

7. Take exercise and get some fresh air during the school day. Do some serious exercise once a week. Teaching makes you feel very tired but exercise will give you more energy, and you function better all round if you keep fit.

8. Plan some 'me' time. Do whatever makes you feel better. This might be soaking in a hot bath, reading novels or watching escapist films.

9. Keep talking to other new teachers (don't forget email or the TES online staffroom) – nobody can understand better than people at the same stage.

10. Invest some time and attention in friends, loved ones and family: they need you and you need them.

Your voice

Sounding a little husky? Is your throat feeling sore? Don't just think it goes with the job; these ailments need to be taken seriously. How you're feeling – depressed, sad, stressed, nervous – comes out in your voice and will affect your teaching unless you put on that jolly, smiley teacher voice. Your voice is your greatest asset, but not using it well can cause lasting damage. One patient in nine at voice clinics is a teacher, and some people are forced to leave the profession after suffering permanent damage to their vocal cords.

Teachers use their voices as much as the busiest professional actor, but do so hour after hour, day after day, and often without any training. Graham Welch, professor of music education at the University of London's Institute of Education, says: 'Voice management is a critical element of successful teaching. When people understand how the voice works, they can use it better' (Bubb, 2005b). Speech is produced when breath passes over your vocal cords, causing them to vibrate. The sound is amplified by the cavities in your chest, mouth and head, and your lips, teeth and tongue shape the sound into recognisable words.

Breathing is fundamental to powering the voice. Deep regular breathing from the diaphragm – in through the nose, out through the mouth – helps you stay calm and works wonders for the voice. When you're stressed and dashing around, you just snatch shallow breaths into your mouth or chest and your tummy doesn't move at all. This means there's not enough power to project the voice, so you strain the weak muscles around your neck and put too much pressure on the vocal cords. Poor posture and tense shoulders and neck mean that the passage of air is blocked.

Tension restricts your voice and can cause lasting damage. The voice is a product of the muscular and breathing systems, both of which suffer when you are stressed, so the ability to relax is essential. Excessive or forceful coughing and throat clearing put great strain on your voice and are often habits rather than physical necessities. Constantly placing demands on the voice – shouting, speaking forcefully or speaking above the pupils and speaking or singing when the voice is tired or sore – is damaging. So is continuing to speak with a sore throat, using maskers such as painkillers, throat sweets or sprays that provide temporary relief. Whispering is just as harmful as shouting because it strains the voice.

Some people damage their voices badly. You should seek medical advice for

- a hoarse voice which persists;

- change in vocal quality, pitch, sudden shifts in pitch, breaks in the voice;

- vocal fatigue for no apparent reason;

- tremors in the voice;

- pain while speaking;

- complete loss of voice.

Roz Comins of Voice Care Network UK (www.voicecare.org.uk) says that many problems are caused by long-established bad habits that can be remedied when accurately diagnosed: 'One teacher wore a brace for three years when she was a teenager and had got used to speaking with her lips barely open to disguise it'. Everyone knows that dehydration is bad for the body but if you're speaking a lot you need to drink even more water because you're constantly losing vocal tract surface lubrication through evaporation. Classrooms can get very hot, dusty and stuffy as well as germ-ridden so keep an eye on ventilation and humidity.

Record yourself teaching for just ten minutes – are you using enough intonation to keep attention, unnecessarily repeating things, talking over the pupils, or simply talking too much? If you really need to shout, do you yell the first word (from the diaphragm, mouth wide open) and then quieten down: 'STOP what you're doing and look this way'? Do you have to talk so much? The look, the smile, the glare, the raised eyebrow, the tut can be so much more effective than words – and so can a theatrical silence or closing of a book.

Do you do warm-ups before the daily onslaught? As you set up your room, practise counting up to 20, starting off with a monotonous voice and then gradually becoming over-excited. This will make the rest of your body come alive. Doing some gentle humming at different pitches, stretching those mouth and face muscles and practising some tongue twisters will really set you up for a day's talking. Use your mouth, lips, teeth and tongue for clearer articulation. We can all fall into habits of mumbling and throwing words away which means that pupils don't hear what we're saying.

Think of all the strategies you can use to engage your pupils that don't involve your voice. Consider body language, signals and gesture; where you position yourself; as well as encouraging and developing pupils' listening skills. For more volume without shouting, fuel your voice with long deep breaths – you should feel your diaphragm moving your stomach – and project your voice. Breathe in a relaxed, focused manner, avoiding lifting shoulders and upper chest. Drink more water: six to eight glasses of still water a day. Drinking tea, coffee, fizzy drinks or alcohol dehydrates the body. If you need to shout, shout the first word then quieten down. Lower the pitch to sound more authoritative. Inhale steam to relax a tired or sore throat. Don't cough to clear your throat too often – swallow or yawn instead. And find someone to massage your neck and shoulders to relax. Hmm, nice…

Managing your time

How many hours a week are you working? It's a good idea to keep track because, let's be honest, you could work 24 hours a day for seven days a week and still find more to do. The risk of burn-out is very real. The profession is haemorrhaging people leaving within the first five years of getting qualified teacher status – because of workload. You, as the new generation of teachers, need to make this job manageable so that you stick with it and enjoy it. You've come into the profession at an ideal time to reap the benefits of research, campaigns and legislation aimed at reducing teachers' workload and improving work–life balance. You shouldn't be doing any of the 24 admin tasks such as display, photocopying and exam invigilation; covering for colleagues should be a rare event; and if you're on induction you should have a ten per cent reduced timetable and ten per cent of that freed up for planning, preparation and assessment (PPA).

But something's wrong because every new teacher I meet seems to be working very long hours. On 5 October 2006 – a month into the job – about 90 primary school NQTs in Lambeth totted up how many hours they'd worked in the last week. Half of them were working more than 60 hours! That's three times as long as they are teaching for – about 20 hours a week. One in ten had worked over 70 hours and two people had clocked up over 80 hours. Yet, in the same room and getting paid the same were a few people who were managing to get the job done in about 48 hours.

That enormous disparity doesn't make sense, on all manner of levels. With a take-home pay of about £1410 a month, people working 50-hour weeks get about £7 an hour but those working 80-hour weeks have an hourly rate of about £4.50. Working long hours is not only financially crazy, but also bad for your health and well-being. As Estelle Morris said when she was Secretary of State for Education, 'A tired teacher is not an effective teacher'. If you don't get enough sleep, noisy classrooms are unbearable. When you're tired, you over-react to minor irritations and end up with even more problems on your hands.

Activity 1.2

Complete Table 1.1 for one week. Add up the time you work at school, at home (on school matters) and while travelling including thinking about school.

Table 1.1 Keeping track of the hours you work (Bubb and Earley, 2004: 64)

	Working at school	Working at home	Travel (work)	Sleep
Sun				
Mon				
Tues				
Weds				
Thurs				
Fri				
Sat				
Total				

In the last week I worked .... hours.

Do you know how many hours you work? The average working week for classroom teachers is 52 hours, but that disguises a wide variation: nearly a fifth work over 60 hours and around 5 per cent do under 40 hours. Having completed Activity 1.2, are you shocked at how many hours you work? Is there any way that travel time can be reduced by, say, going to work or college before the morning rush hour and leaving before the evening one starts? If you use public transport, could you get anything done in travel time – marking, planning, thinking, some 'me' time reading, or a quick nap? A journey can be a good way to wind down after a day's work. For those of you with dependants at home, travelling may be the only time you get to yourself.

Look at what eats up more time than it should. In *Managing Teacher Workload* (Bubb and Earley, 2004) there are charts that show averages for large groups of teachers at different levels and phases. Planning, assessment and making resources are the usual offenders. But simply adding up the amount of time you spend on tasks tells you nothing about how exhausted or frustrated certain tasks – such as sorting out a fight or unblocking the photocopier – can leave you.

Set some limits to your working day and specific tasks. Think about the quality of your time as well as the quantity available. About 20 per cent of a working day is prime time and, used well, should produce 80 per cent of your best work. The rest of your time will be nowhere near as productive, so it's worth recognising which part of the day is best for you and maximising it to get something demanding done rather than flogging yourself when you're tired. The trick is to prioritise so that the essential things get done, and so that what doesn't get done has minimal consequences. Ask your induction tutor and other colleagues what needs a Rolls-Royce effort and what can make do with a Ford Fiesta. Don't be a perfectionist – 'good enough' will do.

Staying strong

Teaching is tough and all teachers need to build up their resilience and stay strong in the face of self doubt. But who knows what disasters life will throw at you during your first year of teaching? As I write, I know of a new teacher who's been diagnosed with breast cancer, another who's caring for her teenage sister while her mother is in the final stages of a terminal illness and a third whose sister died of sudden heart attack. Read the account below (Activity 1.3).

Activity 1.3

Advice on a troubled year

Whether you're a new teacher, induction tutor, coordinator or mentor, think what you would have done in this situation, and what you can learn from this real-life story.

What questions would you ask of the head, mentor and NQT and what advice would you give them? Should the appropriate body (AB) have had a role in this case?

> My first job was at a school miles away from my house. For the first few weeks everything seemed fine although the hour-and-a-half each way spent on public transport was beginning to take its toll. In late September, I was shocked to find that I was pregnant. I miscarried at 10 weeks and ended up having time off work. People at school appeared to be quite supportive but when I returned, everything seemed to change. I

Activity 1.3 continued

was observed within a week and informed that my lesson was unsatisfactory. I found my mentor very difficult to speak to: I would feel ten times worse after a meeting. I began to doubt my abilities as a teacher, even though during my PGCE year I'd been given extremely good feedback.

Things came to a head when my mentor discovered some comments I'd made about how I was feeling on a website forum for NQTs and presented them to the Headteacher. I hadn't posted under my real name or made any derogatory remarks but some of the details made it obvious who I was. I was feeling very low and the website was a real life-line but I was informed that my comments could be viewed as defamatory and that this was a professional conduct issue.

Somehow I muddled through my first term assessment but was told I was 'just tipping the bar'. This was very demoralising. Things rapidly spiralled downwards; I would cry every day and spend hours working in the evenings and at weekends, usually unproductively because I was so worried about making a mistake. I handed in my notice and was due to leave at the end of the spring term, but one Monday morning I woke up and couldn't stop sobbing. I went to see my doctor. I was diagnosed as suffering from stress, anxiety and mild depression. I tried to return to school but it was simply too difficult: my doctor signed me off work and I never went back.

At the time I was worried that I would never recover or return to teaching. I worked as a supply teacher to rebuild my confidence and was offered a permanent position teaching in a local school. One year on, I have just completed my induction and am in a job which I love, working with colleagues who are supportive, understanding and helpful. It's been a difficult time but I learned a lot. It's so important to find a school that's right for you, and even when things get difficult it is possible to turn them around if you persevere. (Anonymous teacher)

Coping with difficult people

> I spend every day at work around people who do not listen, have no respect, answer back, are rude, obnoxious, sometimes just plain stupid ... and then there are the kids! (Induction tutor)

There are lots of fantastic people in schools who are more than happy to share their expertise with and look after new teachers. But every now and then you may be on the receiving end of behaviour that is less than helpful or encouraging. One new teacher said that he was prepared for difficult pupils but finds that he can't cope with some of the other teachers:

> They are arrogant, rude, demanding, unappreciative, uncooperative, back-stabbing, insulting, horrible, horrible human beings and they mean every word of it! (NQT, Term 2)

I'm afraid to say that some people find it hard to switch off from the sort of assertiveness needed to manage a class and they treat their fellow professionals like recalcitrant adolescents. Despite being a great, insidious and difficult issue, few people are doing much about it other than sweep it under the carpet. I hope it helps that I'm bringing it out in the open by saying that not all people who work in schools are the caring, sensitive little bunnies one might wish for. So what do you do when someone upsets you? Well, don't let it get to you too much. Assertiveness training is well worth considering – even if you just read a book on it. There are four behaviour choices that you have in dealing with difficult situations. You can be:

- aggressive – behaviour that makes the other person angry, resentful, hurt or demoralised;

- passive – backing down, withdrawing;

- manipulative – hints, flattery, etc.;

- assertive.

Of all these, assertiveness is usually the most helpful. It's the direct and honest expression of feelings, needs and opinions that calls for self-respect and respect for others. When you're assertive people know where they stand with you – and neither you nor they will get upset. Being aggressive or passive takes a lot out of you, whereas you can feel an inner calm if you're simply assertive. Killing rudeness with kindness is a super strategy.

But look out for behaviour that moves from the inconsiderate to bullying, something that is not unheard of among staff in schools, as the number of cases reported to the TSN indicates. One NQT is scared of her headteacher, who has

> *demanded that everything in my classroom be moved around and wants me to do it on a Saturday; decided to take over as my mentor because my current one has become a friend; told me she has evidence she could fail me on (but can't show it to me); criticises me for things that happen in every other classroom; told other members of staff that she hasn't managed to 'break me' yet; and doesn't let me leave before 5.00pm (NQT, Term 2)*

The largest group of callers to www.bullyonline.org has consistently been teachers. Bullying is defined by the Industrial Society as 'improper, offensive and humiliating behaviour, practices or conduct, which may threaten a person's job security, create an intimidating, unwelcome or stressful work environment, or cause personal offence or injury'. The Stress Management Society identifies two types of bully:

- someone who needs to put others down in order to raise their own self esteem. …

- someone who is overloaded or stressed, and whose tension 'leaks' out as aggressive behaviour. They may be unaware that their actions are perceived as bullying. (http://www.stress.org.uk, accessed May 2007)

The second type is more common but the first is more dangerous. A run-in with a bully can cause stress, damaged self-esteem, depression and even suicide – so don't suffer in silence. Bullying has a destructive effect on confidence, morale and health – all things that are essential requirements in the classroom. The bullied teacher performs less and less well. Stress can cause physical ill-health, such as weight loss, disrupted sleep patterns, nausea, crying fits, indigestion, irritable bowel syndrome, headaches, back pains, skin complaints, ulcers, depression and panic attacks.

You may be the last to realise that you are being bullied. You feel stressed, but put this down to the pressures of dealing with pupils. Often other people notice bullying, as this teacher shows:

> *I witnessed some subtle but very effective bullying of a NQT last year. She was really dynamic, but all her energy was crushed by the head of department. She would come out with some great idea or interesting discussion topic, and was either ignored or cut out of the conversation she had started herself!* (Induction tutor)

So, what can you do? People tell me harrowing stories, but then say 'I don't want you to do anything'. They're worried about making matters worse. Keep a record of incidents, noting down how you were made to feel, and what you did to address any issues raised. Speak to someone you can trust, including the TSN and your union. You may well find out you are not the only one who has suffered. Whatever you do, don't put up with it. Support is available from the following sources:

- The Teacher Support Network (www.teachersupport.info). Phone 08000 562 561 in England or 08000 855 088 in Wales.

- Tim Field's Bully OnLine is at www.successunlimited.co.uk and provides comprehensive information on bullying in the workplace.

- The Andrea Adams Trust (www.andreaadamstrust.org) is a UK charity devoted to raising awareness of and tackling bullying.

- The UK National Work Stress Network (www.workstress.net) aims to identify and eradicate organisational factors that create workplace stress.

- The Stress Management Society (www.stress.org.uk) outlines research on the roots of bullying and the cost of the stress it causes to individuals and employers.

- Check trade union websites, too: National Union of Teachers (www.teachers.org.uk), National Association of Schoolmasters Union of Women Teachers (www.nasuwt.org.uk) and Association of Teachers and Lecturers (www.atl.org.uk).

Keeping happy

Happy teachers make for happy children, but it may be something that you have to work at because your first year is tough. Here are some ideas:

1. Think about all the nice kids you teach.

2. Remember what you were like two months ago. Loads of things will be better.

3. Write 10 good things about your job. Read your list whenever you need cheering up.

4. Identify what you like best – and do more of it! If you enjoy running a drama class after school, see what other opportunities there are for using your skills.

5. Be enthusiastic (even if you don't feel it!). It's infectious, so people react more positively to you and you'll begin to feel genuine job satisfaction. Try not to fixate on the things you don't like about your job, and make it a rule to stop moaning about what's wrong with your work situation.

6. Identify your personal 'pick-me-ups'. If you're feeling a bit flat, do the things that you know will cheer you up. Chocolate and alcohol aren't good for you, so maybe play some upbeat music, chat to a friend or go for a walk.

7. Plan a holiday or two (you have 12 weeks!). What are you going to be doing at half-term, Easter, Whitsun and the glorious summer?

8. Invest in a social life. Feeling that you haven't got one is a sure-fire way to make you feel demotivated: you're supposed to work to live, not live to work.

9. Look for the good in everyone in school – pupils and staff. Avoid gossip.

10. Nominate someone for a Teaching Award. It takes no time at all to do so at www.teachingawards.com. Just write why you think a headteacher, teacher or teaching assistant deserves to win a Teaching Award. Wouldn't it be lovely if somebody nominated you! Yes, there is a category called The Training and Development Agency for Schools' Teaching Award for Outstanding New Teacher. Each of the UK's 14 regions has a winner and then there's an overall winner. Go for gold!

CHAPTER 2

Understanding induction

- ■ What is induction?

- ■ Induction in Scotland and Wales

- ■ Induction in England

- ■ What are NQTs entitled to?

- ■ What happens if you fail induction?

- ■ Who should do induction?

- ■ Where can you undergo induction?

- ■ Models of completing induction

- ■ Roles and responsibilities

What is induction?

> *I don't really understand what the induction period is for, or how it can be passed or failed. Who exactly decides if you are fit to pass your induction period and using what criteria? (NQT, Term 2)*

The first year is the most formative period in a teacher's career, and support is crucial if teachers are to develop the competencies, confidence and attitudes that will keep them happy and successful in the job. Induction should ensure that professional and career development has a firm foundation because it gives new teachers opportunities to become successful in teaching and begin to make a real impact on school development.

Activity 2.1

Test your knowledge

How much do you know about induction already? Try answering this little quiz before you read any further, and then again when you reach the end of this chapter to see if you can raise your score. The answers are peppered throughout this chapter but also listed at the end.

1. Can NQTs do induction without registering with the appropriate General Teaching Council (GTC) and an appropriate body?

2. What are the three elements of induction?

3. How often should NQTs be observed?

4. How often are reports submitted on NQTs?

5. What should NQTs do during the 10 per cent reduced timetable?

6. How long can NQTs do short-term supply?

7. Where must, might and can't NQTs do induction?

The regulations and support covering the first year of teaching vary depending on which part of Great Britain you work in. England has had statutory induction since May 1999, Scotland changed from a two-year to a one-year probationary period in August 2002, and Wales made induction compulsory from September 2003. Figure 2.1 compares the rules for the three countries. Most of the information in this chapter refers to England: different rules apply in Scotland and Wales and information can be found from their GTCs, but here is a brief overview.

Table 2.1 The first year: differences between England, Scotland and Wales

	England	*Scotland*	*Wales*
First year called	Induction	Probation	Induction
No. passed in 2005–06	25,858	2,905	1,542
No. failed in 2005–06	22	9	0
You're known as a	NQT	New teacher or probationer	NQT
Arrangements started	May 1999	August 2002	September 2003
Lead organisation	General Teaching Council for England	General Teaching Council for Scotland	General Teaching Council for Wales
Timetable reduction	10%	30%	10%
Who looks after you	Induction tutor	Supporter	Induction tutor
Time for their job	None	0.1	None
Judged against	Core standards	The Standard for Full Registration	The End of Induction Standard
Assessment	3 times	2 times	3 times
How to get a job	You find it	You are placed in a school for a year	You find it
Time limit between QTS and induction	None	3 years but should do probation straight away	5 years
More info	www.tda.gov.uk	www.gtcs.org.uk	www.gtcw.org.uk

Induction in Scotland and Wales

Scotland

New teachers are given provisional registration with the General Teaching Council for Scotland (GTCS). They have to complete probation and meet the Standard for Full Registration (GTCS, 2006). In 2005–06, 2,905 passed probation: 57 were extended and nine failed. In response to previous difficulties in finding long-term posts, there are two ways to do probation: the Teacher Induction Scheme which takes a year; or the Alternative Route which takes up to 270 days or four terms. Only those people who finish their training in Scotland are guaranteed a one-year new teacher post and a place on the Teacher Induction Scheme, but they have to take these up straight after qualifying unless there are extenuating circumstances. Deferment isn't possible, except on grounds such as needing maternity leave. The placement is for one year, but there's no guarantee that you'll be able to stay afterwards. Probationers are allocated to one of the 32 local authorites and then to a school. You can't choose a local authority, let alone a school: you nominate five authorities you'd consider working in, or you can waive that choice in return for £6,000. The new teacher I met was posted to Orkney, where she was very isolated and the only teacher of her secondary subject on the island!

New teachers on the TIS are generously given a 70 per cent timetable – the rest is for professional development, which consists of core experiences that the authorities organise, and individual activities. Each new teacher has a special 'supporter' who has a role similar to the induction tutor in England. This person has half a day each week to meet and observe the new teacher. Assessment forms are completed twice a year. The standards on which new teachers are judged cover rather more extensive areas than those in England. For instance: 'Registered teachers convey an understanding of practice and general educational matters in their professional dialogue and communication' (GTCS, 2006). The whole system seems very tightly organised, with specific paperwork to be completed.

People who trained outside Scotland can do probation through the Alternative Route only if they have a provisional registration with the GTCS (the application process is rigorous), but they aren't guaranteed a new teacher post and jobs aren't that easy to find.

Wales

In Wales, induction is seen as part of early professional development over the first three years, something which is already in place in Northern Ireland. Otherwise the system closely resembles England except that induction became statutory in Wales for new entrants from September 2003. In March 2006, there were 1,542 NQTs out of 38,498 teachers in the country. NQTs are assessed on the 'Induction Standard'. Anyone failing will be given the opportunity to retake induction: this is certainly a softer approach than England's 'zero tolerance of failure'. There is an appeal system: in 2006 one person went to appeal and lost.

Induction in England

With about 36,000 teachers being awarded QTS every year (Table 2.2) and 25,000 new teachers completing induction, England has the largest and the most embedded induction arrangements. Induction was brought in on 7 May 1999. Its predecessor, the probationary year, was abolished in 1992. For the seven years between 1992 and 1999 there was neither any assessment of the first year of teaching nor a requirement for schools to provide induction. It was up to the 'professional integrity of heads, teachers and advisers to sustain and encourage good practice' (Bleach, 1999: 2). The Department for Education and Skills' guidance on induction, *The Induction Support Programme for Newly Qualified Teachers* (DfES, 2003a), is available online at www.teachernet.gov.uk/professionaldevelopment/induction. The statutory requirements which underpin the induction guidance are Section 19 of the Teaching and Higher Education Act 1998 as amended by Section 139 of the Learning and Skills Act 2000, the Education (Induction Arrangements for School Teachers) (Consolidation) (England) Regulations 2001 and amendments.

Table 2.2 Numbers awarded QTS (General Teaching Council for England (GTCE), 2006b: 6)

QTS awarded by GTCE	2005–06	2004–05	2003–04
Initial teacher training	28,288	27,606	27,283
Flexi PGCE	893	600	649
Graduate and Registered Teacher Programme	4,808	5,039	3,487
Scotland	215	215	198
N. Ireland	57	65	47
European Economic Area	1,319	938	899
Overseas trained teachers	1,163	906	969
Total	36,743	35,369	33,532

The induction period lasts for a school year, which in most cases means that it will start in September and end in July. This is three terms or the part-time equivalent. NQTs are protected from 'unreasonable' demands such as curriculum co-ordination and especially demanding behaviour problems. They have an individualised programme of support, monitoring and assessment from an induction tutor, and objectives are set to help meet the standards for the induction period. There are assessment meetings and reports at the end of each of the three terms. For those who don't do well in their first year, the consequences are draconian: people who fail induction in England are never allowed to teach in maintained schools or non-maintained special schools again. Extensions are allowed only in special cases such as being absent for more than 30 days, and these are awarded by the appropriate body (AB) – the local authority or the Independent Schools Council Teacher Induction Panel (ISCTIP). See below for more information on the AB role.

The induction circular says that:

- Induction combines an individualised programme of monitoring and support, which provides opportunities for NQTs to enhance the knowledge skills they developed when meeting the standards for the award of QTS, with an assessment of their performance. (DfES, 2003a: para. 6)

The key words are: *monitoring, support* and *assessment*. In practice, this means that there is an entitlement for NQTs that should last throughout their induction period. Table 2.3 shows how the support, monitoring and assessment can be balanced over the year.

Table 2.3 Overview of the induction process

	Support	Monitoring	Assessment
Term 1 first half	Week 1 or 2: Complete Transition Point 2 of the Career Entry and Development Profile by discussing the objective(s) needed to help meet the standards, bearing in mind how the new teacher was just before achieving QTS (Transition Point 1) and looking at the current context.	Observation within first 4 weeks	
	Draw up an action plan for meeting the objective(s), including professional development activities (reflection, observing, reading, discussing, study, courses, etc.) to do in the NQT's reduced timetable and meetings with the induction tutor and other staff.	Review progress	
second half	Continue with action plan of professional development activities (reflection, observing, reading, discussing, study, courses, etc.) and meetings, reviewing progress against objectives and changing them as necessary.	Observation	Assessment meeting at end of term. Form for Term 1 completed and sent to AB.
Term 2 first half	Set new objectives, changing them as necessary. Continue with action plan of professional development activities (reflection, observing, reading, discussing, study, courses, etc.).	Observation Review progress	
second half	Continue with action plan of professional development activities (reflection, observing, reading, discussing, study, courses, etc.) and meetings, reviewing progress against objectives and changing them as necessary.	Observation	Assessment meeting at end of term. Form for Term 2 completed and sent to AB.
Term 3 first half	Set new objectives, changing them as necessary. Continue with action plan of professional development activities (reflection, observing, reading, discussing, study, courses, etc.) and meetings.	Observation Review progress	
second half	Continue with action plan of professional development activities (reflection, observing, reading, discussing, study, courses, etc.), reviewing progress against objectives and changing them as necessary. Discuss the questions raised in Transition Point 3 to lead into performance management and continuing professional development.	Observation	Final assessment meeting at end of term to judge whether NQT has met the standards. Form completed and sent to AB.

What are NQTs entitled to?

Under induction NQTs should have the following support, monitoring and assessment:

1. A ten per cent lighter teaching timetable than other teachers in the school. This time is for professional development.

2. A job description that doesn't make unreasonable demands – you shouldn't have to teach exceptionally difficult kids, subjects or age groups that you haven't been trained for, nor should you have a management role.

3. An observation of your teaching within the first four weeks with oral and written feedback, and then every six to eight weeks. You should be observed at least six times throughout the year.

4. Regular meetings with a trained induction tutor, in order to:

   (a) set objectives (with action plans) to help you meet the core standards informed by regular analysis of your strengths and areas for development starting by discussing Transition Point 2 of your career entry and development profile;

   (b) draw up an individualised programme of support, monitoring and assessment;

   (c) review progress before or just after each half-term break (every six or seven weeks).

5. An individualised programme of support, monitoring and assessment.

6. An assessment meeting and report which gets sent to the AB at the end of each term.

7. Procedures to air grievances at school and AB levels.

What happens if you fail induction?

> *I have just realised for the first time that if you fail, you are never allowed to teach again. I don't think this is made very clear to enough people, which is outrageous.* (NQT, end of Term 2)

Under the Education (Induction Arrangements for School Teachers) (Consolidation) (England) Regulations 2001, if your head and AB have evidence that you do not meet the standards by the end of the induction period, you fail. This means that you are no longer eligible to be employed as a teacher in a maintained school or non-maintained special school, ever again. You can't retake induction. Nor can you redo QTS because it isn't taken away; so, you can still call yourself a teacher and would be able to teach in an independent school or work as a private tutor. You could work abroad but not in any of the countries within the European Economic Area (EEA) because of member states' mutual recognition of qualifications.

The good news is that the failure rate is tiny, as can be seen in Table 2.4: in the last three years only 87 have failed while 74,000 have passed induction, so the chances of disaster are about 850:1. However, others jump before they're pushed, but nobody knows quite how many.

Table 2.4 Induction results (GTCE, 2006b: 6)

Induction	2005–06	2004–05	2003–04
Passed	25,858	25,216	22,955
Extended	109	185	148
Failed	22	41	24

You can appeal against the decision that you have not successfully met the standards or a decision to extend your induction period. This is stressful and quite a rigmarole with tight timelines such as submitting your grounds for appeal with supporting evidence within 20 days of being told officially that you've failed induction – that's four weeks of the summer holidays! You'll need strong union representation. The GTC, which hears induction appeals, can:

- allow the appeal;

- dismiss the appeal;

- extend the induction period for as long as it sees fit (which could mean substituting a different extension for the one originally proposed).

The outcomes of these appeals are shown in Table 2.5. Of the 36 appeals by new teachers that came to an outcome (many appeal processes aren't completed), 15 were dismissed, only one was allowed and the others resulted in an extension. Annex D of the induction guidance has information about the employment consequences of failing.

Table 2.5 Induction appeals (GTCE, 2006b: 8)

Induction appeals	2005–06	2004–05	2003–04
Appeal allowed	–	1	–
Appeal dismissed	3	7	5
Extension: 1 term	2	1	1
Extension: 2 terms	2	3	4
Extension: 3 terms	4	2	1
Total	11	14	11

Who should do induction?

> I've just received a letter from the GTC saying that I should not be working as a qualified teacher because I haven't passed all my skills tests! (NQT, Term 2)

People can do induction as soon as they have qualified teacher status and a job for at least a term in a maintained school. Being fully qualified means that they will have passed all the QTS standards – which in England includes the three skills tests in literacy, numeracy and information and communications technology (ICT) – and have a certificate from the GTC. You can't be a member of the GTC until you have QTS, which you'll normally receive in the summer holidays. A typical timeline goes something like this:

- *Mid-June.* Exam board sits. You're told whether you've passed your PGCE or not.

- *End of June/early July.* Training course finishes. Course leader sends off recommendations for QTS to GTC and DCSF. If you haven't passed the skills tests, this can't happen.

- *August.* Your QTS certificate arrives (keep it safe) and with it an application to join the GTC. Send it off straight away because teaching in the state sector without belonging to the GTC is illegal.

- *September.* Start induction, even if you have been employed by a school since July.

If someone begins induction without QTS then the period won't be recognised – nor can it be recognised retrospectively. New teachers who haven't passed their tests should contact the TDA Skills Test team as soon as possible so that they can arrange to take the tests.

Skills tests

I've been employed as a NQT since September but haven't yet (April) passed the numeracy skills test. Am I going to be in trouble? (NQT, Term 3)

Well, in a word, yes! In order to get QTS everyone has to meet standard Q16 – the skills tests. They're hyped up to be worse than they are, and you'll be fine if you practise enough at www.tda.gov.uk/skillstests. Numeracy is the one that most people find toughest, but 81% pass first time and only one in ten people have to have more than two tries. You can have as many goes as you need so don't allow yourself to worry until you're on your third attempt. I know that's no comfort to those of you who go to pieces in tests, don't feel very confident at maths/literacy/ICT, aren't brilliant with computers, especially an unfamiliar one, and would prefer to be tested with a pencil and paper. Prepare, practise and put them into perspective: compared with teaching children every day, they're just a minor inconvenience.

When I said 'minor inconvenience' I was referring to the tests themselves, but it's quite a palaver registering and booking them. They're taken online at designated centres. You may as well book to take all three tests on the same half day because the literacy and numeracy tests run for 45 and 48 minutes respectively and the ICT test takes 35 minutes. If English isn't your first language or if you have a disability such as dyslexia or a visual impairment, register as such – you'll get more time.

Book the tests early to allow time for re-sits well before the end of your course, because no matter how perfectly you pass all other elements you can't get QTS until the tests are passed. Even if you have a teaching job, if the tests aren't done and dusted by the time you start, make clear to the school that you're unqualified. The head might decide not to employ you. One thing's for sure, you can't start induction because to do so you need to be qualified and registered with the GTC. So – (to adapt that handy abbreviation) JFDI – just flipping do it!

You can't do England's induction in a school abroad apart from Service children's schools in Germany and Cyprus, or Guernsey, Jersey, Gibraltar and the Isle of Man. Under the mobility laws, teachers who trained within the EEA (which consists of all members of the European Union plus Iceland, Liechtenstein and Norway) or Switzerland can access teaching positions in the same way as 'home' trained teachers once their qualifications are recognised by the GTC. Teachers who trained outside the EEA need to get QTS in England within four years through the Overseas Trained Teacher Programme. They can apply to be assessed for exemption from induction at the same time as induction if they've been teaching for more than two years in this country or elsewhere. For more information go to www.tda.gov.uk.

Teachers can do induction while working part-time: it takes the equivalent of a school year or 189 days. There's a handy induction calculator on the TDA website. Thus, if someone works two and a half days a week, their induction period will last for six terms. It should start as soon as teachers have a contract for at least a term, even if this is in the middle of a term.

Where can you undergo induction?

Schools must register with what's known as an 'appropriate body' (AB), which can be either the local authority or ISCTIP. See below for more information on the AB role.

Schools that can provide an induction period are:

(a) maintained schools;

(b) non-maintained special schools;

(c) independent schools, if they teach the National Curriculum;

(d) sixth-form colleges.

Schools that can't provide induction include:

(a) pupil referral units;

(b) schools requiring special measures unless one of Her Majesty's Inspectors certifies in writing that the school is suitable for providing induction;

(c) independent schools that don't teach the National Curriculum;

(d) early years settings that are not schools.

You don't have to complete induction in one school (though obviously there are huge advantages in doing so) but each separate period of service should be at least one term long. People can take a break between the terms that make up the induction period, but if the break is longer than five years, they can apply to the relevant AB to seek an extension from the outset of their fresh start.

Independent schools

Induction is optional in the independent sector, though teachers would need to complete induction if they moved to the state sector no matter how experienced. However, they can complete their induction period in an independent school if it teaches the National Curriculum and if the school registers with an AB. Independent schools can use either the local authority AB or ISCTIP.

Sixth-form colleges

Sixth-form colleges can, but don't have to, provide a new teacher with the statutory induction programme. They should ensure that the NQT has a timetable of no more than 90 per cent of normal average teaching time to allow induction to take place. After this, the rules get more complex – and off-putting! No more than 10 per cent of teaching should be devoted to teaching classes of pupils predominately aged 19 and over, and NQTs should spend the equivalent of at least ten school days teaching pupils of compulsory school age. It is recommended that sixth-form colleges should make every effort to provide 20–25 school days' experience in a school setting if that is possible. A new teacher serving induction in a sixth-form college must have an induction tutor who holds QTS.

Supply teaching

Newly qualified teachers in England can do only four terms of short-term supply teaching before passing induction. Short-term supply is anything that is less than a term. The clock starts ticking from the first day's work as a qualified teacher – it's not four terms' worth of work. This can be very hard on people who live in areas where there are very few jobs. When the four terms expire, they must get a post where they can do induction. ABs can extend the four-term limit in exceptional circumstances. If a supply teacher is going to be in a school for a term (even if they're part-time) they must be on induction and the school has to support, monitor and assess as it would any other NQT.

Models of completing induction

In England, induction can be done in several different ways as illustrated in Table 2.6. Jed illustrates the most usual way to do it: starting in September and going through to July in the same school. Some people start in January, and Bea's experience illustrates this. She started teaching a reception class in January and completed induction in the following December. A small number of people start induction after the Easter holidays, as illustrated by Tim's experience.

Table 2.6 Models of completing induction

	Autumn 1	Autumn 2	Spring 1	Spring 2	Summer 1	Summer 2	Autumn 1	Autumn 2	Spring 1	Spring 2
Jed	Induction term 1	Induction term 1	Induction term 2	Induction term 2	Induction term 3	Induction term 3				
Bea			Induction term 1	Induction term 1	Induction term 2	Induction term 2	Induction term 3	Induction term 3		
Tim					Induction term 1	Induction term 1	Induction term 2	Induction term 3	Induction term 3	Induction term 3
Hak		Induction term 1	Induction term 1	Induction term 2	Induction term 2	Induction term 3	Induction term 3			
Jan	PT Induction term 1	PT Induction term 1	PT Induction term 1	PT Induction term 1	PT Induction term 2	PT Induction term 2	PT Induction term 2	PT Induction term 2	FT Induction term 3	FT Induction term 3
Amy	Short-term supply	Sch A Induction term 1	Induction term 1	Short-term supply	Sch B Induction term 2	Induction term 2	Sch C Induction term 3	Induction term 3		
Ed	Induction term 1	Induction term 1	Induction term 2	Induction term 2	Short-term supply	Short-term supply	Induction term 3	Induction term 3		
Oli	Short-term supply	Short-term supply	Short-term supply	Short-term supply	Short-term supply	Short-term supply	Short-term supply	Short-term supply	Can't work unless on induction	
Jo	1 day supply	0	0	0	0	0	0	0	Can't work unless on induction	
Tom	3 days' supply	Travelling	Travelling	Travelling	Travelling	Travelling	Travelling	Travelling	Extension refused	Can't work unless on induction

People who don't make good progress during induction sometimes choose to leave their school after one or two terms. Ed left his school after two terms because his first and second assessment reports outlined problems in his teaching and suggested he would not meet the standards by the end of the year. He spent the summer term doing short-term supply and, having learnt lessons and gained confidence, he started his third term on induction at a new school in September. Things went much better and he completed induction successfully at Christmas.

Induction doesn't have to be started at the beginning of the term but as soon as someone has a term's contract in a school. For instance, Hak started induction on 1 November and completed induction at the end of October in the following school year. Assessment forms were completed in February, May and October rather than at the end of term.

People can complete induction while working part-time, as illustrated by Jan's experience. She worked 0.5 for four terms, thus completing two induction terms' worth and then went full-time for another term. Induction can be done a term at a time, and so possibly in three different schools with or without breaks in between. Amy's experience illustrates this. She did supply for the first half term and after the half-term break got taken on until February, meaning that she could do one term's induction. After working on supply in March, she got another term's post in a different school for the summer term so she was able to complete her second term on induction by the end of July. She successfully applied for another post for the autumn and finished her induction year at the end of December.

Oli did short-term supply for four terms, after which he had to find a post for at least a term so that he could do induction. Jo did only one day's work in September but her time limit ran out at Christmas the following year. Tom did a few days' work on supply then went travelling for over a year. However, he was unable to do any short-term supply work on his return because the four-term limit had expired. He applied for an extension but was turned down. He struggled to find a job with a contract for a term or more where he could start his induction period.

Roles and responsibilities

It's essential that everyone is clear about roles and responsibilities in induction: NQTs, ABs, headteachers and induction tutors are the key players, although I think everyone in a school and indeed the whole education system should be involved and feel responsible.

NQTs

New teachers should take an active role in all aspects of the induction process. They should:

(a) make their CEDP available to the school;

(b) work with their induction tutor to set objectives for professional development and devise an action plan;

(c) engage fully in the individualised induction programme of monitoring, support and assessment, taking increasing responsibility for their professional development;

(d) monitor their progress towards the core standards;

(e) raise any concerns they have about their induction monitoring, support and assessment (based on DfES, 2003a).

Knowing the AB's, headteacher's and induction tutor's responsibilities will also help. But what can new teachers do when their school doesn't play by the rules? In theory they tell the AB, but in practice who is going to complain about their assessor – the head and induction tutor – when these people can recommend a fail? The induction system assumes that all headteachers and ABs know what they're doing and are reasonable people. Unfortunately, some NQTs wouldn't see it like that!

Appropriate Body

Every school has an appropriate body which, among other things, makes the final decision about who passes induction. All local authorities act as AB for state schools. Independent schools can use either the local authority AB or ISCTIP. Statutory duties of AB are as follows:

(a) to ensure that headteachers and governing bodies are aware of and capable of meeting their responsibilities for monitoring, support and guidance;

(b) to ensure their headteachers are capable of undertaking rigorous and fair assessments of NQTs;

(c) to make the final decision about whether an NQT meets the standards for the completion of the induction period and communicate their decision to NQTs, schools and the DCSF/GTC;

(d) to keep records and assessment reports on NQTs;

(e) to provide a named person for NQTs to contact if they are unhappy with schools' support, monitoring and assessment;

(f) to extend the induction period in exceptional circumstances;

(g) to ensure that schools with NQTs get any earmarked funding (DfES, 2003a).

Headteachers

The headteacher of a school with someone undergoing induction has key responsibilities:

(a) to ensure that each NQT has an individualised induction programme;

(b) to make a recommendation to the AB, based on rigorous and fair assessment procedures, as to whether the NQT has met the standards for induction;

(c) to designate an induction tutor for each NQT who is adequately prepared and is able to work effectively in the role (the headteacher may be the induction tutor);

(d) to ensure that any duties assigned to the NQT are reasonable;

(e) to ensure that NQTs are provided with a timetable representing no more than 90 per cent of the average contact time normally allocated to more experienced teachers in the school, and that the time released is protected, is distributed throughout the induction period and used for professional development;

(f) to observe any NQT at risk of failing to meet the standards, and inform the AB (based on DfES, 2003a).

Headteachers are contractually obliged to give NQTs a 10 per cent lighter timetable than other class teachers in the school on top of PPA time, which is 10 per cent of teaching contact hours. Contact hours do not include assembly, break and lunchtimes or time spent on pastoral activities. For more information on PPA time, go to www.teachernet.gov.uk.

Induction tutors

The induction tutor has day-to-day responsibility for monitoring, support and assessment. They should be appropriately experienced and have regular contact with the NQT. In many primary schools the induction tutor will be the deputy head or a phase coordinator. In a secondary school there are normally at least two levels of support – the head of department and a senior member of staff, as can be seen in Table 2.7. NQTs should be clear about who does what.

Support is key to the success of the induction year. NQTs may need colleagues to take a range of roles: planning partner, colleague, friend, supporter, counsellor, assessor, helper, disciplinarian of pupils, adviser, critical friend, facilitator, motivator, expert practitioner, organiser, monitor of progress, trainer, protector and parent. Clearly, an induction tutor couldn't and shouldn't take on all these roles. The whole staff is responsible for inducting a new teacher. Table 2.7 shows how different schools have arranged induction support. Induction tutors are responsible for the following:

(a) making sure that NQTs know and understand the roles and responsibilities of everyone involved in induction. Many schools now have an induction policy that gives clear guidance, particularly about everyone's rights and responsibilities;

(b) organising, in consultation with NQTs, a tailored programme of monitoring, support and assessment (see Table 2.8 for example);

(c) coordinating and carrying out lesson observations and the follow-up discussions;

(d) reviewing progress against objectives and the core standards;

(e) ensuring that dated records are kept of monitoring, support, and formative and summative assessment activities (based on DfES, 2003a).

Table 2.7 Organisation of induction personnel (Bubb *et al.*, 2002: 29)

<u>Primary School 1 (mono-support)</u>	
Induction tutor	Member of the senior management team
<u>Primary School 2 (mono-support)</u>	
Induction tutor	Headteacher
<u>Primary School 3 (bi-support)</u>	
Induction tutor	Member of the senior management team
Mentor	The parallel class teacher
<u>Primary School 4 (tri-support)</u>	
Induction Coordinator	Member of the senior management team
Induction tutor	Year group leader
Buddy mentor	A recently qualified teacher
<u>Secondary School 1 (mono-support)</u>	
Induction tutor	Senior member of staff
<u>Secondary School 2 (bi-support)</u>	
Induction coordinator	Senior member of staff in charge of all NQTs
Induction tutor	The head of department
<u>Secondary School 3 (tri-support)</u>	
Induction coordinator	Senior member of staff in charge of all NQTs in the school
Induction tutor	The head of department
Buddy mentor	A recently qualified teacher
<u>Secondary School 4 (tri-support)</u>	
Induction tutor/coordinator	A senior teacher who organises the induction programme, meetings, assessment reports, etc.
Academic mentor	The head of department who advises on all subject-related matters
Pastoral mentor	A head of year who gives guidance on behaviour management and pastoral issues
<u>Secondary School 5 (multi-support)</u>	
Staff development officer	In charge of coordinating the induction programme for all NQTs and organises contracts, job descriptions, staff handbook and the pre-induction visits before the NQTs start work
Subject mentor	Head of the department that the NQT works in, supervises planning and teaching and gives subject specific input
Pastoral mentor	A head of year who gives guidance on behaviour management and pastoral issues
Buddy mentor group	A group of recently qualified teachers who provide day-to-day informal support

Table 2.8 Julian's induction programme Term 1

Objectives for Term 1:
1. To engage more pupils in learning more of the time through improved organisation, planning and behaviour management
2. To communicate effectively with parents and carers conveying information about how their children have settled in.

Monitoring	How NQT spends reduced timetable	Meetings with induction tutor (20 mins)	Staff meetings and school CPD
Week 1	LA induction afternoon – relating to parents & colleagues	Discuss CEDP Transition Point 1	Planning
Week 2	Organise room. Label resources	Classroom organisation	Child protection
Week 3 Observation 1: organisation	Observe Ms A, focusing on organisation	Feedback & discussion following observation Set objectives. CEDP Transition Point 2	Parents' evening arrangements
Week 4	LA induction afternoon – classroom management	Behaviour management	Black History Month
Week 5 Parents eve	Prepare for parents' evening	Parents' evening tips	None
Week 6 Planning monitored	View resources for Black History Month	Monitor planning	Review behaviour policy
Week 7	Observe Mr B, focusing on behaviour	Half-term review Set new objectives	Book scrutiny
Week 8 Book scrutiny – 3 pupils	Observe own class being taught by supply teacher	Book scrutiny feedback (assessment coordinator)	Marking
Week 9 Observation 2: pupil engagement	LA induction afternoon – special needs	Post-observation discussion	Behaviour policy
Week 10	Observe own class being taught by induction tutor	None	Anti-bullying policy
Week 11	Teachers TV programmes	Discuss Teachers TV programmes	Festival arrangements
Week 12	Self-review against the standards	Assessment meeting. Review and set objectives	IEP reviews
Week 13	None	Assessment report	None

The induction tutor needs to be fully aware of the requirements of the induction period and to have the skills, expertise and knowledge needed to provide or coordinate effective guidance and support, and to make rigorous and fair judgements about performance in relation to the core tandards. Thus induction tutors, like mentors of trainee teachers, will have specific professional development needs. Local authorities, higher education institutions and consultancies run varying degrees of training, and some of the longer and more in-depth courses are accredited. Many of the skills required of initial teacher training mentors and induction tutors are the same – observation, feedback, coaching, report writing. However, the similarities can disguise the differences, and a lot is at stake for NQTs who do not meet the standards, so it is important that induction tutors have the necessary skills, expertise and knowledge.

More than anything, NQTs value someone who wants to support them and can give them time. This is a very precious resource as induction tutors often have many other time-consuming roles and their time spent on induction is rarely funded. As ever, much has to be done on goodwill or it doesn't happen. Here are positive comments that a group of NQTs made about their induction tutors.

1 *They were always available for advice.*

2 *They gave me a regular meeting time, even though they were busy.*

3 *They were genuinely interested in how I was doing.*

4 *They were honest and open, which encouraged trust.*

5 *They listened to me – and didn't impose their own views.*

6 *They made practical suggestions.*

7 *They shared their expertise, ideas and resources.*

8 *They were encouraging and optimistic – they made me feel good.*

9 *They stopped me working myself into the ground by setting realistic objectives.*

10 *They weren't perfect themselves, which was reassuring!*

11 *They looked after me, keeping parents and the Head off my back.*

12 *Their feedback after observations was useful. Good to get some praise and ideas for improvements.*

13 *It helped when they wrote the end-of-term reports because these gave us a clear picture of how we were doing.*

14 *They were well organised, and if they said they'd do something they did it. (Bubb, 2000: 14)*

Answers to Activity 2.1

1. NQTs must be registered with the GTC and appropriate body (AB).

2. The three elements of induction are support, monitoring and assessment.

3. NQTs should be observed within the first four weeks, then every six to eight weeks.

4. Assessment reports are written at end of each term.

5. The 10 per cent reduced timetable is for continuing professional development (CPD).

6. There's a four-term limit to short-term supply.

7. NQTs *must* do induction in all maintained and non-maintained special schools on a term's contract. They *could* do (optional) induction in sixth-form colleges; the independent sector; schools in Jersey, Guernsey, Isle of Man, Gibraltar; and Service children's schools in Cyprus and Germany. Induction *can't* be done in any school with less than a term's contract; schools in special measures unless Her Majesty's Inspectorate agrees; settings that don't have school status; pupil referral units; further education colleges; or schools abroad

CHAPTER 3

The standards

- The framework of teacher standards
- How induction tutors can use the standards for their development
- The core standards
- Tricky issues

Pity the poor people who have been induction tutors since induction has been statutory, because in eight years there have been three different sets of standards. From 1999, NQTs had to meet the QTS standards plus ten extra for induction. Then things changed in 2003. There were new QTS standards and six different induction standards. There was yet another complete change in 2007, with 41 core standards that new teachers have to meet.

The framework of teacher standards

Since September 2007, there's been a coherent framework of professional and occupational standards for classroom teachers, designed by the Training and Development Agency for Schools (TDA). As you can see in Table 3.1, there are standards for qualified teacher status (Q), the core standards that NQTs must meet (C) and which form the basis of the post-threshold (P), excellent teacher (E) and advanced skills teacher (A) standards, all of which are underpinned by the five key outcomes for children and young people identified in *Every Child Matters* (DfES, 2003b) and the six areas of the *Common Core of Skills and Knowledge for the Children's Workforce* (DfES, 2005). I've also included the 12 standards for Chartered London Teacher (CLT) status that you can work towards if you're employed in any of the city's 33 local authorities.

Table 3.1 The framework of professional standards for teachers in England (based on TDA, 2007b)

Those recommended for the award of QTS (Q) should:	All teachers (C) should:	Post-threshold Teachers (P) should:	Excellent teachers (E) should:	Advanced skills teachers (A) should:
1. Professional attributes				
Relationships with children and young people				
Q1 Have high expectations of children and young people including a commitment to ensuring that they can achieve their full educational potential and to establishing fair, respectful, trusting, supportive and constructive relationships with them.	**C1** Have high expectations of children and young people including a commitment to ensuring that they can achieve their full educational potential and to establishing fair, respectful, trusting, supportive and constructive relationships with them.			
Q2 Demonstrate the positive values, attitudes and behaviour they expect from children and young people.	**C2** Hold positive values and attitudes and adopt high standards of behaviour in their professional role.			
Frameworks				
CLT 11 Promote and implement policies and practices that encourage mutual tolerance and respect for diversity, challenge discrimination and widen pupils' understanding of their contribution to society.				
Q3 (a) Be aware of the professional duties of teachers and the statutory framework within which they work.	**C3** Maintain an up-to-date knowledge and understanding of the professional duties of teachers and the statutory framework within which they work, and contribute to the development, implementation and evaluation of the policies and practice of their workplace, including those designed to promote equality of opportunity.			
(b) Be aware of the policies and practices of the workplace and share in collective responsibility for their implementation.		**P1** Contribute significantly, where appropriate, to implementing workplace policies and practice and to promoting collective responsibility for their implementation.	**E1** Be prepared to take a leading role in developing workplace policies and practice and in promoting collective responsibility for their implementation.	**A1** Be prepared to take on a strategic leadership role in developing workplace policies and practice and in promoting collective responsibility for their implementation in their own and other workplaces.

Those recommended for the award of QTS (Q) should:	All teachers (C) should:	Post-threshold Teachers (P) should:	Excellent teachers (E) should:	Advanced skills teachers (A) should:
Communicating and working with others				
		CLT 4 Progress partnerships within and beyond the classroom with support staff, teachers, other professionals, agencies and community resources, to promote pupils' achievements, learning, development and well-being. *CLT 9 Promote and apply shared professional learning and other forms of support and development for teachers to learn and work together, taking account of teacher mobility, to strengthen collective knowledge and expertise across teachers in London.*		
Q4 Communicate effectively with children, young people, colleagues, parents and carers.	**C4** (a) Communicate effectively with children, young people and colleagues. (b) Communicate effectively with parents and carers, conveying timely and relevant information about attainment, objectives, progress and well-being. (c) Recognise that communication is a two-way process and encourage parents and carers to participate in discussions about the progress, development and well-being of children and young people.			
Q5 Recognise and respect the contribution that colleagues, parents and carers can make to the development and well-being of children and young people and to raising their levels of attainment.	**C5** Recognise and respect the contributions that colleagues, parents and carers can make to the development and well-being of children and young people, and to raising their levels of attainment.			
Q6 Have a commitment to collaboration and co-operative working.	**C6** Have a commitment to collaboration and co-operative working where appropriate.			
Personal professional development				
Q7 (a) Reflect on and improve their practice, and take responsibility for identifying and meeting their developing professional needs. (b) Identify priorities for their early professional development in the context of induction.	**C7** Evaluate their performance and be committed to improving their practice through appropriate professional development.			

Those recommended for the award of QTS (Q) should:	All teachers (C) should:	Post-threshold Teachers (P) should:	Excellent teachers (E) should:	Advanced skills teachers (A) should:
Q8 Have a creative and constructively critical approach towards innovation, being prepared to adapt their practice where benefits and improvements are identified.	C8 Have a creative and constructively critical approach towards innovation; being prepared to adapt their practice where benefits and improvements are identified.		E2 Research and evaluate innovative curricular practices and draw on research outcomes and other sources of external evidence to inform their own practice and that of colleagues.	
Q9 Act upon advice and feedback and be open to coaching and mentoring.	C9 Act upon advice and feedback and be open to coaching and mentoring.			

2. Professional knowledge and understanding

CLT 7 Identify and use the knowledge and experiences that pupils, their families and other communities bring from outside the school to enrich curriculum development and teaching practices.

Teaching and learning

Those recommended for the award of QTS (Q) should:	All teachers (C) should:	Post-threshold Teachers (P) should:	Excellent teachers (E) should:	Advanced skills teachers (A) should:
Q10 Have a knowledge and understanding of a range of teaching, learning and behaviour management strategies and know how to use and adapt them, including how to personalise learning and provide opportunities for all learners to achieve their potential.	C10 Have a good, up-to-date working knowledge and understanding of a range of teaching, learning and behaviour management strategies and know how to use and adapt them, including how to personalise learning to provide opportunities for all learners to achieve their potential	P2 Have an extensive knowledge and understanding of how to use and adapt a range of teaching, learning and behaviour management strategies, including how to personalise learning to provide opportunities for all learners to achieve their potential.	E3 Have a critical understanding of the most effective teaching, learning and behaviour management strategies, and including how to select and use approaches that personalise learning to provide opportunities for all learners to achieve their potential.	

Assessment and monitoring

CLT 5 Analyse and use relevant data to inform and promote the highest possible aspirations for pupils and to target expectations and actions to raise pupil achievements.

Those recommended for the award of QTS (Q) should:	All teachers (C) should:	Post-threshold Teachers (P) should:	Excellent teachers (E) should:	Advanced skills teachers (A) should:
Q11 Know the assessment requirements and arrangements for the subjects/curriculum areas they are trained to teach, including those relating to public examinations and qualifications.	C11 Know the assessment requirements and arrangements for the subjects/curriculum areas they teach, including those relating to public examinations and qualifications.	P3 Have an extensive knowledge and well-informed understanding of the assessment requirements and arrangements for the subjects/curriculum areas they teach, including those related to public examinations and qualifications.		
		P4 Have up-to-date knowledge and understanding of the different types of qualifications and specifications and their suitability for meeting learners' needs.		
Q12 Know a range of approaches to assessment, including the importance of formative assessment.	C12 Know a range of approaches to assessment, including the importance of formative assessment.			

Those recommended for the award of QTS (Q) should:	All teachers (C) should:	Post-threshold Teachers (P) should:	Excellent teachers (E) should:	Advanced skills teachers (A) should:
Q13 Know how to use local and national statistical information to evaluate the effectiveness of their teaching, to monitor the progress of those they teach and to raise levels of attainment.	**C13** Know how to use local and national statistical information to evaluate the effectiveness of their teaching, to monitor the progress of those they teach and to raise levels of attainment.			
	C14 Know how to use reports and other sources of external information related to assessment in order to provide learners with accurate and constructive feedback on their strengths, weaknesses, attainment, progress and areas for development, including action plans for improvement		**E4** Know how to improve the effectiveness of assessment practice in the workplace, including how to analyse statistical information to evaluate the effectiveness of teaching and learning across the school.	

Subjects and Curriculum

CLT 6 Demonstrate ongoing development and application of subject, specialism and/or phase knowledge and expertise, drawing on opportunities and resources in London to enrich the learning experience.

Those recommended for the award of QTS (Q) should:	All teachers (C) should:	Post-threshold Teachers (P) should:	Excellent teachers (E) should:	Advanced skills teachers (A) should:
Q14 Have a secure knowledge and understanding of their subjects/curriculum areas and related pedagogy to enable them to teach effectively across the age and ability range for which they are trained.	**C15** Have a secure knowledge and understanding of their subjects/curriculum areas and related pedagogy including the contribution that their subjects/curriculum areas can make to cross-curricular learning; and recent relevant developments.			
		P5 Have a more developed knowledge and understanding of their subjects/curriculum areas and related pedagogy including how learning progresses within them.	**E5** Have an extensive and deep knowledge and understanding of their subjects/curriculum areas and related pedagogy gained for example through involvement in wider professional networks associated with their subjects/curriculum areas.	
Q15 Know and understand the relevant statutory and non-statutory curricula and frameworks, including those provided through the National Strategies, for their subjects/ curriculum areas, and other relevant initiatives applicable to the age and ability range for which they are trained.	**C16** Know and understand the relevant statutory and non-statutory curricula and frameworks, including those provided through the National Strategies, for their subjects/curriculum areas and other relevant initiatives across the age and ability range they teach.			

Those recommended for the award of QTS (Q) should:	All teachers (C) should:	Post-threshold Teachers (P) should:	Excellent teachers (E) should:	Advanced skills teachers (A) should:
Literacy, numeracy and ICT				
Q16 Have passed the professional skills tests in numeracy, literacy and information and communications technology.				
Q17 Know how to use skills in literacy, numeracy and ICT to support their teaching and wider professional activities.	**C17** Know how to use skills in literacy, numeracy and ICT to support their teaching and wider professional activities.			
Achievement and diversity				
	CLT 10 Build on, extend and apply knowledge of the range of communities, cultures and sub-cultures in London, to inform and promote individual pupils' learning.			
	CLT 12 Demonstrate a capacity to deal constructively and sensitively with conflicting community and cultural values in classrooms and schools.			
Q18 Understand how children and young people develop and that the progress and well-being of learners are affected by a range of developmental, social, religious, ethnic, cultural and linguistic influences.	**C18** Understand how children and young people develop and how the progress, rate of development and well-being of learners are affected by a range of developmental, social, religious, ethnic, cultural and linguistic influences.			
Q19 Know how to make effective personalised provision for those they teach, including those for whom English is an additional language or who have special educational needs or disabilities, and how to take practical account of diversity and promote equality and inclusion in their teaching.	**C19** Know how to make effective personalised provision for those they teach, including those for whom English is an additional language or who have special educational needs or disabilities, and how to take practical account of diversity and promote equality and inclusion in their teaching.			
			E6 Have an extensive knowledge on matters concerning equality, inclusion and diversity in teaching.	
Q20 Know and understand the roles of colleagues with specific responsibilities, including those with responsibility for learners with special educational needs and disabilities and other individual learning needs.	**C20** Understand the roles of colleagues such as those having specific responsibilities for learners with special educational needs, disabilities and other individual learning needs, and the contributions they can make to the learning, development and well-being of children and young people.			
	C21 Know when to draw on the expertise of colleagues, such as those with responsibility for the safeguarding of children and young people and special educational needs and disabilities, and to refer to sources of information, advice and support from external agencies.			

Those recommended for the award of QTS (Q) should:	All teachers (C) should:	Post-threshold Teachers (P) should:	Excellent teachers (E) should:	Advanced skills teachers (A) should:
		Health and well-being		
Q21 (a) Be aware of the current legal requirements, national policies and guidance on the safeguarding and promotion of the well-being of children and young people. (b) Know how to identify and support children and young people whose progress, development or well-being is affected by changes or difficulties in their personal circumstances, and when to refer them to colleagues for specialist support.	**C22** Know the current legal requirements, national policies and guidance on the safeguarding and promotion of the well-being of children and young people.			
	C23 Know the local arrangements concerning the safeguarding of children and young people.			
	C24 Know how to identify potential child abuse or neglect and follow safeguarding procedures.			
	C25 Know how to identify and support children and young people whose progress, development or well-being is affected by changes or difficulties in their personal circumstances, and when to refer them to colleagues for specialist support.	**P6** Have sufficient depth of knowledge and experience to be able to give advice on the development and well-being of children and young people.		

3. Professional skills

Those recommended for the award of QTS (Q) should:	All teachers (C) should:	Post-threshold Teachers (P) should:	Excellent teachers (E) should:	Advanced skills teachers (A) should:
		Planning		
Q22 Plan for progression across the age and ability range for which they are trained, designing effective learning sequences within lessons and across series of lessons and demonstrating secure subject/curriculum knowledge.	**C26** Plan for progression across the age and ability range they teach, designing effective learning sequences within lessons and across series of lessons informed by secure subject/curriculum knowledge.	**P7** Be flexible, creative and adept at designing learning sequences within lessons and across lessons that are effective and consistently well-matched to learning objectives and the needs of learners and which integrate recent developments, including those relating to subject/curriculum knowledge.	**E7** (a) Take a lead in planning collaboratively with colleagues in order to promote effective practice. (b) identify and explore links within and between subjects/curriculum areas in their planning.	
Q23 Design opportunities for learners to develop their literacy, numeracy and ICT skills.	**C27** Design opportunities for learners to develop their literacy, numeracy, ICT and thinking and learning skills appropriate within their phase and context.			
Q24 Plan homework or other out-of-class work to sustain learners' progress and to extend and consolidate their learning.	**C28** Plan, set and assess homework, other out-of-class assignments and coursework for examinations, where appropriate, to sustain learners' progress and to extend and consolidate their learning.			

Those recommended for the award of QTS (Q) should:	All teachers (C) should:	Post-threshold Teachers (P) should:	Excellent teachers (E) should:	Advanced skills teachers (A) should:
	CLT 2 Apply a wide range of teaching and learning strategies to reduce individual barriers to learning and to meet the variety of pupil needs in London. *CLT 3 Develop and implement inclusive practices in a range of learning settings appropriate to the diversity of pupils in London and the complexity of their personal learning, including support for Special Education Needs, to raise pupils' achievements.*			
	Teaching			
Q25 Teach lessons and sequences of lessons across the age and ability range for which they are trained in which they: (a) use a range of teaching strategies and resources, including e-learning, taking practical account of diversity and promoting equality and inclusion. (b) build on prior knowledge, develop concepts and processes, enable learners to apply new knowledge, understanding and skills and meet learning objectives. (c) adapt their language to suit the learners they teach, introducing new ideas and concepts clearly, and using explanations, questions, discussions and plenaries effectively. (d) demonstrate the ability to manage the learning of individuals, groups and whole classes, modifying their teaching to suit the stage of the lesson.	**C29** Teach challenging, well-organised lessons and sequences of lessons across the age and ability range they teach in which they: (a) use an appropriate range of teaching strategies and resources, including e-learning, which meet learners' needs and take practical account of diversity and promote equality and inclusion. (b) build on the prior knowledge and attainment of those they teach in order that learners meet learning objectives and make sustained progress (c) develop concepts and processes which enable learners to apply new knowledge, understanding and skills (d) adapt their language to suit the learners they teach, introducing new ideas and concepts clearly, and using explanations, questions, discussions and plenaries effectively (e) manage the learning of individuals, groups and whole classes effectively, modifying their teaching appropriately to suit the stage of the lesson and the needs of the learners. **C30** Teach engaging and motivating lessons informed by well-grounded expectations of learners and designed to raise levels of attainment.	**P8** Have teaching skills which lead to learners achieving well relative to their prior attainment, making progress as good as, or better than, similar learners nationally.	**E8** Have teaching skills which lead to excellent results and outcomes. **E9** Demonstrate excellent and innovative pedagogical practice.	

Those recommended for the award of QTS (Q) should:	All teachers (C) should:	Post-threshold Teachers (P) should:	Excellent teachers (E) should:	Advanced skills teachers (A) should:
Assessing, monitoring and giving feedback				
CLT 5 Analyse and use relevant data to inform and promote the highest possible aspirations for pupils and to target expectations and actions to raise pupil achievements.				
Q26(a) Make effective use of a range of assessment, monitoring and recording strategies.	C31 Make effective use of an appropriate range of observation, assessment, monitoring and recording strategies as a basis for setting challenging learning objectives and monitoring learners' progress and levels of attainment.			
(b) Assess the learning needs of those they teach in order to set challenging learning objectives.			E10 Demonstrate excellent ability to assess and evaluate.	
Q27 Provide timely, accurate and constructive feedback on learners' attainment, progress and areas for development.	C32 Provide learners, colleagues, parents and carers with timely, accurate and constructive feedback on learners' attainment, progress and areas for development.		E11 Have an excellent ability to provide learners, colleagues, parents and carers with timely, accurate and constructive feedback on learners' attainment, progress and areas for development that promotes pupil progress.	
Q28 Support and guide learners to reflect on their learning, identify the progress they have made and identify their emerging learning needs.	C33 Support and guide learners so that they can reflect on their learning, identify the progress they have made, set positive targets for improvement and become successful independent learners.			
	C34 Use assessment as part of their teaching to diagnose learners' needs, set realistic and challenging targets for improvement and plan future teaching.			
Reviewing teaching and learning				
Q29 Evaluate the impact of their teaching on the progress of all learners, and modify their planning and classroom practice where necessary.	C35 Review the effectiveness of their teaching and its impact on learners' progress, attainment and well-being, refining their approaches where necessary.			
	C36 Review the impact of the feedback provided to learners and guide learners on how to improve their attainment.			
			E12 Use local and national statistical data and other information, in order to provide (a) a comparative baseline for evaluating learners' progress and attainment, (b) a means of judging the effectiveness of their teaching, and (c) a basis for improving teaching and learning.	

Learning environment

CLT 1 Create and manage a classroom environment to ensure a secure and supportive achievement culture and behaviour strategy to meet the needs of London's diverse and mobile pupil population.

CLT 12 Demonstrate a capacity to deal constructively and sensitively with conflicting community and cultural values in classrooms and schools.

Those recommended for the award of QTS (Q) should:	All teachers (C) should:	Post-threshold Teachers (P) should:	Excellent teachers (E) should:	Advanced skills teachers (A) should:
Q30 Establish a purposeful and safe learning environment conducive to learning and identify opportunities for learners to learn in out-of-school contexts.	C37 (a) Establish a purposeful and safe learning environment which complies with current legal requirements, national policies and guidance on the safeguarding and well-being of children and young people so that learners feel secure and sufficiently confident to make an active contribution to learning and to the school. (b) Make use of the local arrangements concerning the safeguarding of children and young people. (c) Identify and use opportunities to personalise and extend learning through out-of-school contexts where possible making links between in-school learning and learning in out-of-school contexts.			
Q31 Establish a clear framework for classroom discipline to manage learners' behaviour constructively and promote their self-control and independence.	C38 (a) Manage learners' behaviour constructively by establishing and maintaining a clear and positive framework for discipline, in line with the school's behaviour policy. (b) Use a range of behaviour management techniques and strategies, adapting them as necessary to promote the self-control and independence of learners.			
	C39 Promote learners' self-control, independence and cooperation through developing their social, emotional and behavioural skills.			

Team Working and Collaboration

CLT 4 Progress partnerships within and beyond the classroom with support staff, teachers, other professionals, agencies and community resources, to promote pupils' achievements, learning, development and well-being.

CLT 8 Contribute to the development and application of whole school policies and activities, to extend opportunities for pupil and school achievements in London.

Those recommended for the award of QTS (Q) should:	All teachers (C) should:	Post-threshold Teachers (P) should:	Excellent teachers (E) should:	Advanced skills teachers (A) should:
Q32 Work as a team member and identify opportunities for working with colleagues, sharing the development of effective practice with them.	C40 Work as a team member and identify opportunities for working with colleagues, managing their work where appropriate and sharing the development of effective practice with them.	P9 Promote collaboration and work effectively as a team member.	E13 Work closely with leadership teams, taking a leading role in developing, implementing and evaluating policies and practice that contribute to school improvement.	A2 Be part of or work closely with leadership teams, taking a leadership role in developing, implementing and evaluating policies and practice in their own and other workplaces that contribute to school improvement.

Those recommended for the award of QTS (Q) should:	All teachers (C) should:	Post-threshold Teachers (P) should:	Excellent teachers (E) should:	Advanced skills teachers (A) should:
Q33 Ensure that colleagues working with them are appropriately involved in supporting learning and understand the roles they are expected to fulfil.	**C41** Ensure that colleagues working with them are appropriately involved in supporting learning and understand the roles they are expected to fulfil.	**P10** Contribute to the professional development of colleagues through coaching and mentoring, demonstrating effective practice, and providing advice and feedback.	**E14** Contribute to the professional development of colleagues using a broad range of techniques and skills appropriate to their needs so that they demonstrate enhanced and effective practice.	
			E15 Make well-founded appraisals of situations upon which they are asked to advise, applying high level skills in classroom observation to evaluate and advise colleagues on their work and devising and implementing effective strategies to meet the learning needs of children and young people leading to improvements in pupil outcomes.	
				A3 Possess the analytical, interpersonal and organisational skills necessary to work effectively with staff and leadership teams beyond their own school.

The framework is arranged in three interrelated sections:

1. Professional attributes

2. Professional knowledge and understanding

3. Professional skills.

The standards are organised like a tree, with the core standards being the trunk off which the other standards grow. Each set of standards builds on the previous set so that, for instance, a teacher aspiring to become an advanced skills teacher (AST) would need to satisfy the standards that are specific to that status (A) as well as meeting the preceding relevant standards (C, P and E).

How induction tutors can use the standards for their development

Many people who work in a mentoring role enjoy it, saying it's the best part of their many roles and they get a lot from it. Until now, however, helping teachers develop has been a rather low-status role with rare financial rewards. The beauty of the framework is that those who support, monitor and assess new teachers can see that their work can be used to demonstrate standards for their promotion, as you can see in those for crossing the threshold:

P1 Contribute significantly, where appropriate, to implementing workplace policies and practice and to promoting collective responsibility for their implementation.

P6 Have sufficient depth of knowledge and experience to be able to give advice on the development and well-being of children and young people.

P10 Contribute to the professional development of colleagues through coaching and mentoring, demonstrating effective practice, and providing advice and feedback.

Progress on the upper pay scale will depend not only on teachers showing that they have developed themselves but also that they are coaching and mentoring less experienced teachers. Induction tutors hoping to gain excellent teacher status will have to demonstrate that they meet standards such as the following:

E14 Contribute to the professional development of colleagues using a broad range of techniques and skills appropriate to their needs so that they demonstrate enhanced and effective practice.

E15 Make well-founded appraisals of situations upon which they are asked to advise, applying high level skills in classroom observation to evaluate and advise colleagues on their work and devising and implementing effective strategies to meet the learning needs of children and young people leading to improvements in pupil outcomes.

When they make the grade, they'll be expected to be involved in:

■ induction of NQTs;

■ professional mentoring of other teachers;

■ sharing good practice through demonstration lessons;

■ helping teachers to develop their expertise in planning, preparation and assessment;

■ helping other teachers to evaluate the impact of their teaching on pupils;

■ undertaking classroom observations to assist and support the performance management process;

■ helping teachers improve their teaching practice including those on capability procedures.

The framework is progressive, reflecting the development of teachers' professional attributes, knowledge, understanding and skills. Post-threshold teachers are expected to act as role models for teaching and learning, make a distinctive contribution to raising standards across the school and provide regular coaching and mentoring to less experienced teachers. At a higher level, ASTs support staff in other schools one day a week and draw on the experience they gain elsewhere to improve practice in their own and other schools.

The core standards

There are 41 core standards for NQTs to meet. This is how they're spread across the three headings:

1. Professional attributes – standards 1–9

2. Professional knowledge and understanding – standards 10–25

3. Professional skills – standards 26–41.

A useful activity for induction tutors and NQTs to do is to analyse the core standards in order to come to a shared understanding of what they mean and what would constitute a satisfactory performance in each one. For instance, there doesn't seem to be much difference between the standards for QTS and induction other than that there are eight more to meet (33 for QTS) and the latter assume that they are being met in an employment context. The ones about safeguarding children illustrate the varying expectations (see Table 3.2).

One might think meeting standards that have already been met would be a straightforward matter. However, what a beginning teacher on a seven-week teaching practice with a stable class in a supportive setting and weekly observations and feedback can achieve may be very different from what the same person can do in their first job. The ease with which teachers meet the core standards will depend on:

- the calibre of their initial teacher training;

- how well the QTS standards were met during training;

- the context of the classes and school;

- the support during the induction period;

- their induction tutor's interpretation of what the standards mean;

- how hard they work and how quickly they learn;

- what happens in their lives during their first year.

Many NQTs work in schools that are very different from those they experienced during their training: by and large, the best schools are used for people to train in, but new teachers are likely to get jobs in places which experienced teachers avoid. Even in the most favourable conditions – where a new teacher works in the school where they spent their teaching practice – things can be very hard. Everyone knows that some classes within a school are harder to teach than others. In addition, there are the problems inherent in joining a new organisation, such as building relationships and understanding the politics of the staffroom.

In contrast, the 27 Northern Ireland competencies (General Teaching Council for Northern Ireland, 2007) recognise that each standard is a continuum to be met to different degrees depending on a teacher's role, experience and context.

Activity 3.1

Analyse the similarities and the differences between the induction and QTS standards relating to safeguarding children in Table 3.2. What will a NQT need to know that a trainee teacher doesn't?

Table 3.2 Safeguarding children: the core and QTS standards

Core standards	QTS standards
C22 Know the current legal requirements, national policies and guidance on the safeguarding and promotion of the well-being of children and young people.	Q21 (a) Be aware of the current legal requirements, national policies and guidance on the safeguarding and promotion of the well-being of children and young people.
C23 Know the local arrangements concerning the safeguarding of children and young people.	
C24 Know how to identify potential child abuse or neglect and follow safeguarding procedures.	
C25 Know how to identify and support children and young people whose progress, development or well-being is affected by changes or difficulties in their personal circumstances, and when to refer them to colleagues for specialist support.	(b) Know how to identify and support children and young people whose progress, development or well-being is affected by changes or difficulties in their personal circumstances, and when to refer them to colleagues for specialist support.

Tricky issues

The 'professional attributes' are the most fundamental of all the standards, I think, and they're the ones which are most difficult to improve. They're based on the GTCE's code of conduct for all teachers. But what about NQTs who don't take responsibility for their development? We've all met people who see training as time off, who think they've nothing more to learn, who are unreflective, and who don't consider how their professional development might affect pupils. They are the ones most likely not to succeed in their induction year.

New teachers have to demonstrate and promote the positive values, attitudes and behaviour that they expect from pupils. Going from being a student to a professional is tough but it's a role change that's absolutely essential to command respect. Because we're always reminding pupils to speak politely and treat people with respect, we need to make sure we behave impeccably. But we're human too: if coffee spills on some important papers, it's hard not to swear. As part of your teacherly persona, you will have probably already invented a range of expletives that make you sound like one of Enid Blyton's Famous Five. But what should you do if something closer to a real swear word escapes from your lips? It's unlikely not to be noticed as young people have finely tuned antennae for such lapses. With a wonderful show of double standards, it's often the serial cursers who most delight in loudly and publicly shaming teachers who swear. The safest thing to do is apologise straight away to anyone who heard, saying that you realise how inappropriate it is. Then let the head or deputy know so that they'll take the wind out of the sails of anyone who tells tales or complains. More ambiguous are phrases that aren't actually swearing but which you would not be entirely happy hearing pupils say, such as 'Stop acting like a prat', 'God!', 'Gordon Bennett', 'Get off your arse' or 'Shut up'? Try to avoid them.

There are some oddities among the standards. Using research findings is expected only of advanced skills and excellent teachers. How crazy! On the other hand, new teachers will have to adopt an open, positive and 'constructively critical approach towards innovation' (C8), which seems unnecessary since everything is fairly new for NQTs, as well as hard to interpret and impossible to judge. In spite of it being new teachers' prime concern, managing behaviour gets few specific mentions. You need to know a range of strategies (C10) and use them to establish and maintain 'a clear and positive framework for discipline', adapting them to promote learners' 'self-control and independence' (C38). Standards of pupils' behaviour vary enormously between schools and even classes. Some schools have more successful behaviour policies and procedures than others. Similarly, the number and range of pupils with special educational needs (SEN) vary enormously between schools and classes. In some there is an enormous number of pupils with complex needs. Undertaking induction in classes with a high proportion of pupils with SEN and the support staff who go with them would be hard and increase the chances of NQTs failing. Success will depend on how good the school's special educational needs coordinator (SENCO) is, the use of outside agencies and the time and help allocated to implementing and reviewing individual education plans (IEPs).

The core standards appear on the surface to be straightforward. It's only when one studies them in detail and tries to imagine what a good, average and unsatisfactory meeting of them would entail that their complexity becomes apparent. In my experience people interpret each standard differently, and have widely differing expectations of what a new teacher should be able to do. Look at this one:

C41 Ensure that colleagues working with them are appropriately involved in supporting learning and understand the roles they are expected to fulfil.

What if you are like 22-year-old Sharon who has to liaise with, deploy and guide the eight SEN assistants and two classroom assistants who work over the week with the five statemented children in her mainstream reception class of 30? The other adults she works with are not only older than she, but are local parents and a formidable gang. Some have very strong views on what they will and will not do. Leading and managing any other staff requires skills and experience, and Sharon has ten to deal with.

The success of an individual NQT depends largely upon the practice in their school. It has always been the case that individual teachers stand a greater chance of being effective in a well-organised school, but for NQTs this becomes even more important. If the school has successful planning and target-setting procedures that all teachers are using, clearly the NQT will be at a huge advantage.

The core standards are very demanding: they describe a perfect teacher rather than someone learning the trade. No one would argue with the need for the highest standards for the education profession, but it seems to me to be like expecting someone leaving medical school to be at brain surgeon level. In a way, that is what NQTs have to be – they are expected to teach a class like the teacher next door who has 20 years' experience. The pupils in both classes deserve the best teaching, but what can we realistically expect of someone at the start of their career? You might think that it'd be more sensible to qualify standards like C3 – 'Communicate effectively with children, young people, . . . parents and carers' – with a phrase such as 'with support'. As Colin Richards, a former schools inspector, wrote:

> *The Standards represent an impossible set of demands which properly exemplified would need the omnicompetence of Leonardo da Vinci, the diplomatic expertise of Kofi Annan, the histrionic skills of Julie Walters, the grim determination of Alex Ferguson, and the saintliness of Mother Teresa, coupled with the omniscience of God.* (Richards, 2000)

High expectations, with standards to aspire to and drive professional development, are great; but since failing to meet the standards at the end of induction results in teachers not being able to teach in state schools ever again, you would think that the criteria for passing need to ensure that only the irredeemably hopeless fail. Most NQTs are at or beyond the level implied by the standards by the end of their first year, but that isn't really the point. If the system is going to fail people for not meeting standards, then the baseline needs to be low or you'll have to fail too many – or resort to pretending they meet them, which is what happens now, causing anxiety and some buck passing ('we won't fail you so long as you leave our school'). If standards were set at a minimum competency level, everyone would agree that those not meeting them should be kicked out of the profession. Surely it's crazy for schools with very high standards to be able to fail an average NQT for not rigorously and consistently meeting every standard.

Unfortunately, the TDA has to date given no definition or description of what someone not quite meeting a standard might look like. While there is probably agreement about what constitutes a very strong passing of the standards, everyone will surely have their own ideas of what is good enough. Perhaps we need a standardised mark scheme! Until there are firmer guidelines some headteachers and ABs with very high standards might fail a NQT who might be passed by others. Without more guidance and moderation, the induction system risks being enormously unfair.

Once all parties are clear about what the standards mean, NQTs' strengths and needs can be identified so that the right support is given, and it is to this that we now turn.

CHAPTER 4

Key concepts to help development

- What is professional development?

- Learning styles

- Experiential learning

- The change equation

- The professional development cycle

- Levels of impact

- Keeping a professional portfolio

- The career entry and development profile

What is professional development?

The Training and Development Agency (2007c) defines professional development as 'reflective activity designed to improve an individual's attributes, knowledge, understanding and skills. It supports individual needs and improves professional practice.' This is a fairly narrow definition. I prefer the definition that Peter Earley and I wrote because it's more wide-ranging and goes well beyond the mere acquisition of knowledge or skills. For us, staff development is:

> an ongoing process encompassing all formal and informal learning experiences that enable all staff in schools, individually and with others, to think about what they are doing, enhance their knowledge and skills and improve ways of working so that pupil learning and well-being are enhanced as a result. It should achieve a balance between individual, group, school and national needs; encourage a commitment to professional and personal growth; and increase resilience, self-confidence, job satisfaction and enthusiasm for working with children and colleagues. (Bubb and Earley, 2007: 4).

Do you know how you learn best? Is it something that you even think about? If you're going to make the most of professional development opportunities, it's an important question because there are many ways to achieve the same end – you need to choose what works for you.

Learning styles

There's been lots of debate about children's learning styles but not much on how to help the adults in schools to learn – and goodness knows there's lots needed with the current pace of change. Thinking about 'andragogy' (how adults learn) is important because, for instance, adults learn best when the topic is of immediate use. Some people consider that adults have preferred learning styles. For instance, Honey and Mumford (2006) identify four different types of adult learners – theorists, pragmatists, activists and reflectors.

Theorists like to learn in structured situations where they're offered interesting ideas and concepts, such as lectures, deep discussions, reading and thinking alone. They learn less when they have to participate in situations that emphasise emotions.

Pragmatists learn best when the topic is of obvious relevance and when shown something they can put into practice. They learn less well when there's no practice or guidelines as to how something is done.

Activists learn best when involved in new experiences, problem-solving, team tasks and role-play. They learn less well when listening to lectures or long explanations; reading, writing, or thinking on their own; absorbing data; or following instructions to the letter.

Reflectors like time to think about the subject such as through lectures with plenty of reflection time; observation; and keeping a learning log/journal to review what has happened. They learn less when role-playing, being thrown in at the deep end or worried by deadlines.

Honey and Mumford's questionnaire aims to help people pinpoint their learning preferences so that they're in a better position to select learning experiences that suit them. Few people fall neatly into one category, but have a leaning towards one or two as I found out when training induction tutors. One was identified through the questionnaire as an activist through and through, with no characteristics of the reflector, pragmatist or theorist. This was an 'aha' learning moment for her because she realised that the advice she'd been giving to her NQT hadn't been working because he was so different from her – strongly a reflector and theorist, with low scores as an activist. So, make sure your induction tutor knows how you learn best.

Experiential learning

Experiential learning is important for adults – the cycle of 'do, review, learn, apply' (Dennison and Kirk, 1990). So, someone who wants to get better at taking assembly, for instance, might usefully go through the cycle in this way:

Do   Observe someoneon whom I admire taking assembly.

Review   Think about it and discuss it with them afterwards.

Learn   Learn some key techniques for taking assembly.

Apply   Try them out when I take assembly.

Do   Get someone to observe me taking assembly and give me feedback.

People learn in different ways and have preferred learning styles but learning takes place in a variety of ways and in different settings. It can be formal or informal, within the workplace or off-site. One can also think of learning in vertical (knowing more, new learning and experiences) and horizontal dimensions (the same knowledge applied in different contexts, deeper understanding). So, teachers don't always have to learn new things to be developing professionally, but at some level they will be changing their practice. This brings me to another idea that I've found useful: the change equation.

The change equation

Experts on managing change in organisations say that this requires vision, skills, incentives, resources and action plans. But I think it works for new teachers too: if any one of those five things is missing, you'll find it hard to develop; Table 4.1 shows some of the consequences. Let's think about Madeleine who has poor behaviour in tutor group time. The chatting and mucking about are getting her down. So she needs:

Vision – knowing how she wants her tutor group to behave

Skills – she has behaviour management skills that she uses successfully when teaching her subject

Incentives – people have complained about the noise the form makes

Resources – advice from colleagues; observation of other teachers' form times; reading articles; time to think through what she's going to do

Action plan – drawing up a plan of what she's going to do and when.

Table 4.1 The change equation (Martin and Holt, 2002: 37)

Vision	Skills	Incentives	Resources	Action Plans	= Change
******	Skills	Incentives	Resources	Action Plans	= Confusion
Vision	******	Incentives	Resources	Action Plans	= Anxiety
Vision	Skills	******	Resources	Action Plans	= Gradual Change
Vision	Skills	Incentives	******	Action Plans	= Frustration
Vision	Skills	Incentives	Resources	******	= False Starts

If she doesn't have a *vision* of how she wants them to behave, she won't develop because she doesn't know what her boundaries for behaviour are in this less formal time. Without the *skills* to improve behaviour, such as rewards and sanctions, she'll get anxious and feel inadequate. If there are no *incentives*, such as people complaining or someone observing her, she may develop but not as quickly. She'll get frustrated if there are no *resources*, such as advice from colleagues, books to read, observation of other people's form times, or time to think through what she's going to do. Without an *action plan*, written or mental, she may not get round to improving things consistently or there'll be lots of false starts.

Now, look at your objectives. Do you have a vision and the skills, incentives, resources and an action plan to improve? Developing is not easy to do so it's useful to have a thorough view of the professional development cycle and think about how adults learn before getting into the nitty-gritty of identifying needs.

The professional development cycle

The professional development cycle consists of six stages, as shown in Figure 4.1. The first two stages are the identification of needs and their analysis, taking into account what teachers already know and can do. The next challenge is to find the best way to meet needs: the range of professional development activities is huge, as we'll see in the next chapter. The final stages in the cycle – monitoring and evaluating the impact of professional development and training – are neglected areas. Monitoring is concerned with checking progress, seeing that things are going according to plan and making alterations if necessary. Gauging the impact of CPD or evaluating its effectiveness on teaching and learning – the sixth and last stage in the staff development cycle – is more difficult but there are plenty of simple examples in the next chapter of how NQTs have put ideas into practice.

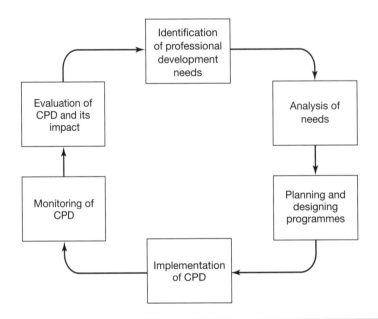

Figure 4.1 The professional development cycle (Bubb and Earley, 2004: 39)

Activity 4.1

Think of a professional development activity you've undertaken. What were you hoping to achieve? What was its impact? For instance, are you more knowledgeable, and if so, in what way?

Levels of impact

Tom Guskey (2002) has done some important work in this field. He identifies five levels of evaluation of CPD with improved pupil outcomes being the desired end result:

1. Participants' reactions

2. Participants' learning

3. Organisation support and change – the key role that the school can play in supporting or sabotaging any development

4. Participants' use of new knowledge and skills

5. Pupil learning outcomes.

Guskey suggests that reversing these five levels can be useful in professional development planning. So begin planning by asking 'What improvements in pupils do I want and how will I know when they're achieved?', and then ask 'If that's the impact I want, what needs to change?'

I've adapted this idea to seven levels of impact:

1. How you felt about the CPD activity while doing it

2. Whether you learned or improved something

3. What organisational support is needed

4. Whether you do something as a result

5. Whether this has an impact on pupils

6. Whether this has an impact on other staff, and in turn, their pupils

7. Whether this has an impact on staff and pupils in other schools.

An example of how this might work in relation to preparing for a parents' evening is shown in Table 4.2.

Table 4.2 **Levels of impact: preparing for a parents' evening**

Levels of impact	Preparing for parents' evening
1. How you felt about the CPD activity while doing it	I observed my induction tutor doing a parent interview. It felt odd and was a bit boring at the time, but it was useful talking about it afterwards.
2. What did you learn or improve?	Yes, I've got strategies for structuring the interview, keeping to time, having notes and a piece of illustrative work.
3. Can the school do anything to help?	The SENCO is going to be with me for my first parent interview.
4. What did you do as a result of the CPD?	I did parents' evening successfully.
5. What impact has this had on pupils?	Too early to say. Parents went away with a clear picture of how their children are doing and I am following up issues raised by three sets of parents.
6. Has there been any impact on other staff, and in turn, their pupils?	No.
7. Has there been any impact on staff and pupils in other schools?	Not yet, but I mentioned my learning to another NQT who is going to set up similar structured support in his school.

Alternatively, you could see different levels of impact like those from Jill's one-day induction tutor training course:

Level 1: Immediate reaction. Despite the day being well organised and in pleasant surroundings, Jill did not enjoy it because she had to sit next to and work with her ex-husband's second wife – the woman her husband left her for!

Level 2: Learning, networks, confidence. However, she gained much new knowledge and increased her skills. She felt more confident in the role of induction tutor. The extensive handouts reminded her of her learning and provided easy-to-use systems.

Level 3: Putting things into practice. Jill used her newly learned knowledge, skills and confidence in working with the two NQTs.

Level 4: Impact on teachers. The NQTs said that the school's induction was initially poor but improved after Jill attended the course. They really noticed a difference because of all the new systems and found their induction very effective. They felt well supported, and monitored and assessed fairly so that they were able to make good progress in their first year.

Level 5: Impact on pupils. This had an impact on the NQTs' pupils who learned more and behaved.

Activity 4.2

What professional development activity has had most impact on you? Why?

Keeping a professional portfolio

Everyone needs somewhere to keep all their induction, professional development and performance management related paperwork. You have lots of folders to do with pupils (plans, assessments, etc.), but things to do with us as teachers need to be kept safely too. All your objectives, action plans, reflections and assessments should be kept in a professional portfolio for your whole career and be used for induction, performance management, threshold and job applications. Your AB or school may give you one, but if not just start one up yourself – not just for your first year but for your whole career. Outside bodies, such as the local authority or Ofsted, may want to look at it, but basically it's for you and not for anyone to check up on. It shouldn't be onerous to keep: Table 4.3 shows a suggested structure. If any parts of a portfolio don't work for you, change them – it's yours!

Table 4.3 The professional portfolio

1. Career history
   (a) CV and qualifications
   (b) CEDP summary of training
   (c) References
   (d) Job descriptions

2. Objectives
   (a) CEDP Transition Point 1
   (b) CEDP Transition Point 2
   (c) Action plans for objectives
   (d) Individualised induction programme, including any courses
   (e) CEDP Transition Point 3

3. Professional development
   (a) Professional development activities and meetings
   (b) Notes from professional development meetings, e.g. with induction tutor
   (c) Handouts and certificates from courses attended
   (d) Notes from observing other staff
   (e) Articles read and websites visited
   (f) List of networks made

4. Evidence of effectiveness
   (a) Copy of the framework of teacher standards
   (b) Professional review meeting (at half-term)
   (c) Monitoring of teaching (e.g. at least six observations)
   (d) Assessment forms (end of each term on induction)
   (e) Evidence of standards

5. Other information
   (a) Policies for induction, CPD and performance management
   (b) Information about advanced skills and lead teachers

In Scotland, systems are tighter. Evidence of professional development during the probationary year period has to be gathered into a comprehensive CPD portfolio and used beyond probation. The contents are not optional but listed as:

- a copy of your timetable, detailing the 6.75 hours (0.3 full-time equivalent) of CPD undertaken each week and the variety of experience gained in the 15.75 hours (0.7 full time equivalent) of teaching

- your self-evaluation overview and initial teacher education profile

- the professional development action plan allowing you to identify CPD requirements

- CPD tracking record plus any additional details of CPD experiences you have undertaken and your evaluation of them

- supporter meeting notes

- observed teaching feedback form

- supporting evidence, discussed in how to meet the Standards for Full Registration, including plans and materials used during observed teaching sessions and in other CPD experience

- a copy of your interim profile and final profile. (www.gtcs.org.uk)

Some people keep portfolios electronically: your school may use software such as Sims, Blue or Ascon that you can slot into. The DCSF has developed a free electronic portfolio called *Keeping Track* (www.teachernet.gov.uk), which provides teachers with the opportunity to build and maintain an e-portfolio. Once you've logged in, using a password, all of the information is kept in the site confidentially but you can print off a copy of documents. There is much on this website for NQTs and induction tutors to dip into and use selectively. The templates section has CVs, questionnaires, self-audits, and a learning journal, that you can use or modify.

The career entry and development profile

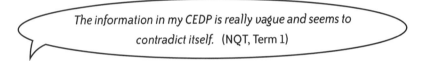

The information in my CEDP is really vague and seems to contradict itself. (NQT, Term 1)

The career entry and development profile was introduced in summer 2003, replacing the career entry profile. The CEDP gives some structure to teachers at key milestones in their professional development: towards the end of their initial training programme and at the start and end of their induction period. It refers to these milestones as 'transition points', and using the profile will help teachers to make constructive connections between these points. New teachers are given a CEDP near the end of their training, and its purposes are:

- to be a connection from ITE to effective professional practice

- to focus reflection on achievements and goals

- to guide the processes of discussion and reflection about professional development needs (TDA, 2007a).

It is not a record of evidence towards meeting the core standards. The CEDP assumes that the NQT will have a professional portfolio – there are no sheets for objectives. In fact, I suggest that you transfer the main contents (there's lots of padding) to your portfolio so that everything is kept together.

The CEDP consists of a summary of training and then questions for reflection on strengths and areas for development at 'transition points':

- Transition Point 1 is completed with the tutor responsible for training, just before the award of QTS.

- Transition Point 2 is completed with the induction tutor at the start induction.

- Transition Point 3 is completed with the induction tutor towards the end of induction.

Go to www.tda.gov.uk/teachers/induction/cedp for more detail.

Towards the end of their training new teachers should discuss these Transition Point 1 questions with someone who knows their work:

1. At this stage, which aspect(s) of teaching do you find most interesting and rewarding? What has led to your interest in these areas? How would you like to develop these interests?

2. As you approach the award of QTS, what do you consider to be your main strengths and achievements as a teacher? Why do you think this? What examples do you have of your achievements in these areas?

3. In which aspects of teaching would you value further experience in the future? For example:

   ■ aspects of teaching about which you feel less confident, or where you have had limited opportunities to gain experience;

   ■ areas of particular strength or interest on which you want to build further.

   At the moment, which of these areas do you particularly hope to develop during your induction period?

4. Do you have any thoughts at this stage about how you would like to see your career develop?

You need to show the CEDP and TP1 to your induction tutor as soon as you can. Discuss your training, teaching practices and the sorts of classes and schools you encountered. Mention other relevant experience you have gained. Remember that your induction tutor may not have seen your application form. Your strengths and areas for development need to be discussed carefully so that the induction tutor knows exactly to what they refer. Understanding the context of the final teaching practice that the comments were based upon is all important. You then need to discuss Transition Point 2 once you and your induction tutor have an idea of your new context – so, after a week or two.

Transition Point 2 asks about your professional development priorities during induction:

1. At the moment, what do you consider to be your most important professional development priorities during your induction period?

2. How have your priorities changed since Transition Point 1?

3. How would you prioritise your needs across your induction period?

4. What preparation, support or development opportunities do you feel would help you move forward with these priorities?

Consider aspects of teaching that you'd like more experience in – because they're strengths or interests, weaknesses or areas of limited experience. What are your longer-term aspirations? How do you want your career to develop? Many people are happy just to be teaching, but others have a clear career plan. For instance, you may want to become a team leader or educational psychologist, and so would want to be gaining relevant experience. Break your priorities down into those for the short, medium and long term. Reflect with your induction tutor on why they are priorities and note down what help you need, from whom and when. These can then be turned into objectives for you to work on – and this is the subject of the next chapter.

Analysing needs, setting objectives and drawing up action plans

- Analysing needs

- Setting an objective

- Drawing up action plans

- When a new teacher is struggling

Analysing needs

Identifying learning needs is important because it really isn't that easy. Identifying needs can be done superficially, with people saying what they want rather than what they need – or why. Most people benefit from a real and accurate analysis in order to get the help they need. For instance, does someone with control problems need a behaviour management course? Perhaps, but in my experience problems with behaviour are the symptom of something else: the root cause might be to do with planning, relationships, attitude, organisation or expectations.

It's very hard to decide what to work on when things are not going right, because each problem has a huge knock-on effect – and some NQTs have suffered from not having areas for development accurately diagnosed. Particularly when someone has a problem, it needs to be reflected upon and analysed in order to draw up the most useful objectives and plan of action. These steps are useful in analysing development needs:

1. *Brainstorm the problem's features.* It's good to look at exactly what the problem is and its consequences. For instance, new teacher Annie's control problems included the following:
   - Her voice is thin and becomes screechy when raised.
   - Sometimes she comes down hard on the pupils and at other times she lets them get away with things.
   - She takes a long time to get attention.
   - She runs out of time so plenaries are missed, the class is late to assembly, etc.

- Pupils call out.
- Pupils are too noisy.
- A small group of pupils is behaving badly.
- Even the usually well-behaved pupils are being naughty.

When you've made the list, look at it. Does it seem a fair picture? It's easy to be too hard or too generous.

2. *List some positive features* relating to the problem area. For instance, Annie:
    - really likes and cares for the pupils;
    - speaks to them with respect;
    - plans interesting work for them;
    - is very effective when working with individuals or small groups;
    - works hard and has better control in the early part of the day.

3. *Reflection time.* Think about why things go well – reflection on successes is very powerful. For instance, Annie realised that things were better in the mornings because she was fresher and when she had a teaching assistant with her. The process of analysing strengths is very helpful and this positive thinking can now be used to reflect on problems. It's important to diagnose the reasons for the problem – the root cause. For instance, rather than saying that 'noisy pupils cause Annie problems', be more diagnostic: 'noise causes Annie to overstretch her voice, which compromises her authority'. Test out your hypotheses with the teacher and anyone else who can comment.

Setting an objective

Once needs have been analysed, it's useful to encapsulate what to develop into some sort of objective or target. This will provide a framework for doing a complex job at a very fast pace. Setting an objective encourages you to prioritise, be realistic, make best use of time and other resources, and feel a sense of achievement when small steps are made. The very act of writing an objective down forces you to consider whether it is the real priority and gives you something to focus on. Induction tutors could ask questions to structure the setting of an objective, as is shown in Table 5.1.

Michael Tidd, a new teacher in West Sussex, enjoys setting a mix of targets: a few of the 'I'm not very confident in this' type but also an 'I'm fairly knowledgeable about such-and-such, but I'd really like to develop that further' one. He trained to teach Key Stages 2 and 3 and got interested in the whole area of how schools help or hinder young people managing transitions. So, one of his objectives that builds on this strength is to increase liaison between his middle school and the local high schools to examine the continuity of the Key Stage 3 curriculum.

A frequent problem with objectives is that they're not made specific enough – 'I want to be a better teacher' – which can lead to failure. Objectives should be SMART:

- Specific

- Measurable

- Achievable

- Relevant

- Time-bound.

Table 5.1 Questions to structure the setting of an objective

Questions	Examples of answers
What would you like to improve?	Challenging higher attainers.
Why? What's the current picture? (What's the evidence?)	Observation, work samples and my gut feeling show that higher attainers could be doing better. Some mess around and avoid working.
How will you know that things have improved?	Higher attainers will be engaged in lessons and will produce good work.
What do you need to do to meet this objective?	Plan more challenging work. Raise expectations of what they can achieve.
	Develop my questioning skills so that I can really get them thinking. Where possible, set them purposeful problems to solve.
	Seize opportunities for pupils to extend themselves, e.g. competitions or projects.
What professional development will help you?	Discuss with gifted and talented coordinator.
	Find ideas from websites such as www.londongt.org.
	Read and use Bloom's taxonomy of questioning.
	Observe two teachers (one in present school, one in another) with a reputation for challenging higher attainers, and discuss strategies.
How should your progress and its impact be monitored?	Keep track that activities happen by the date agreed.
	In the third week of March, observe a lesson and look at the work of three pupils to see impact.

An objective such as 'Improve control' may be too large. It's better to be more specific about what needs most urgent attention. For Annie this was: 'To improve control, particularly after playtimes, in independent literacy activities, at tidying-up time, and home-time within a half-term'. Is that specific, measurable, achievable, relevant and time-bound? I think so.

It's useful to think about how you will know whether things are better in a year's time: aim high, but be realistic. These points then become the success criteria around which you draw up an action plan of what needs to be done when. Think of actions to remedy situations – they can be surprisingly easy. It's often the small things that make a difference.

Drawing up an action plan

Once you've chosen an area to develop, you need to decide how you're going to do so – and draw up an action plan with dates. What budget or time allocation is there? You may think there's none, but ask around. All schools have to meet their staff development needs and there should be money, time and resources available. Choose something that's going to work for them within the timescale, whether it's reading a book, watching Teachers TV, going on a course or observing someone's lesson.

Annie completed a very detailed action plan (see Table 5.2). Such detail is not always necessary, though it illustrates how breaking a problem into manageable chunks helps. For her, these were:

- to get attention more quickly;

- to shout rarely;

- to plan for behaviour management;

- to set up procedures for sorting out disputes after playtimes, tidying, hometime, and independent literacy activities.

Table 5.2 An action plan to meet an objective: improving control*

Name: Annie   Date: 10 Sept.   Date objective to be met: 19 Oct.

Objective: To improve control, particularly after playtimes, in independent activities, at tidying-up time, and hometime.

Success criteria	Actions	When	Progress notes
Pupils will know what the class rules are	Write class rules with the children and discuss why they're important. Display prominently. Refer to them when individuals are sticking to the rules and when they're breaking them	11 Sept.	*12 Oct. Working well. Children remind each other sometimes!*
I will get attention more quickly	Brainstorm attention-getting devices with other teachers. Use raised hand	15 Sept.	
I will rarely shout	Voice management within NQT course Project the voice Don't talk over children	29 Sept.	*19 Oct. Using more range in voice – working!*
I will have 20 strategies for rewarding good behaviour	Brainstorm (with other teachers) ways to respond to positive and negative behaviour. Order them in terms of	26 Sept.	*8 Oct. Working well when I remember but when I'm tired I'm more inclined to nag!*
I will have 20 strategies for responding to poor behaviour	positiveness (a treat) and negativity (leave the room). Remember to use light touch responses to negative behaviour and plenty of responses to good behaviour and ask teaching assistant to, as well. Ask teaching assistant to give me feedback on how I'm doing		
There will be procedures for sorting out disputes after playtimes	Glean ideas from other teachers Ask playground supervisors to note serious incidents Children to post messages in incident box	11 Oct.	*18 Oct. Incident box really working for those who can write and I can now tell when there's a serious problem.*
Tidying will be done more quickly	Discuss and observe what other teachers do Start tidying earlier and time it with reward for beating record. Play a track of music – all to be finished by the end!	18 Sept.	*25 Sept. Working well though still a few children not helping. Might try minutes off playtime.*
There will be procedures for hometime	Observe and discuss ideas with other teachers Monitors to organise things to take home Start hometime procedures earlier and time them (with rewards?)	25 Sept.	*12 Oct. Changed routine so tidy earlier. Some Year 6 children helping give out things to take home.*

*See Template 1 in the Appendix for a blank version.

Her professional development didn't cost much: one course on voice management and lots of observation and discussion. The impact, however, was great because the CPD was so finely tuned to solving problems with managing behaviour.

Writing annual reports to parents is another area guaranteed to overwhelm even the most organised of new teachers, so there's an action plan in Table 5.3 that you could adapt for your own purposes by putting in dates appropriate to your situation.

Table 5.3 An action plan to meet an objective: reports (See Template 1 in the Appendix for a blank version)

Name: Date:	Date objective to be met:		
Objective: Write annual reports to parents that give a clear picture of children's progress and achievements.			
Success criteria	*Actions*	*When*	*Progress*
You have an evidence base - i.e. you know what each child can do	Collate assessment information so that you know what each child can do in the key aspects of every subject. Gather information from other teachers if necessary. Fill gaps in knowledge of what the class can do. Give pupils a self-assessment so that you have insight into what they think they've learnt and their greatest achievements.		
You know what the school expects.	Find out the school system for writing reports – speak to the assessment coordinator. Read some examples that have been identified as being good. Note stylistic features and key phrases.		
You have written one report to an acceptable standard	Read the children's previous year's report. Write one child's report in draft. Give to the headteacher for comment.		
You have a timetable that will enable you to meet the deadline.	Set up the system for reports (i.e. computer format). Draw up a timetable of when you're going to write the reports, allowing about two hours for first five, one hour for next twenty, three quarters for last five, one-third over half-term. Liaise with other teachers who are contributing to the reports.		
You meet the deadline	Write the reports. Give them to the headteacher for checking and signing. Celebrate!		
Review			

When a new teacher is struggling

I know it's fashionable to say that less is more, but when it comes to action plans I think detail really helps: breaking tasks into bite-sized chunks helps and makes you feel as though you're making progress. Where a new teacher is struggling it's even more important to diagnose the problem and put into action a detailed plan. In the example in Table 5.4, the induction tutor, the head of department and the SENCO were involved in different aspects. The induction tutor and SENCO focused on the improvement and implementation of behaviour strategies while the head of department concentrated on the teaching and learning strategies. No class will behave if the work's boring! Everyone kept records of all the support and monitoring they did and all notes of meetings and lesson observations were signed and dated by the NQT and whoever else was present. Copies of all paperwork were kept in folders by both the induction tutor and NQT.

Table 5.4 An action plan to meet an objective: behaviour (See template in the appendix for a blank version) (based on Bleach *et al.*, 2004: Appendix 4.3)

Name:	Date:	Date objective to be met:		
Objective:	To implement appropriate behaviour strategies so that all pupils behave well and make satisfactory progress throughout the lesson			
Success criteria	*Actions*		*When*	*Progress*
Use a range of strategies to establish and maintain the satisfactory behaviour of pupils throughout lessons. All pupils will be on task throughout lessons and make appropriate progress.	1. NQT is asked to read the school behaviour policy and note issues causing difficulty or areas which need further guidance 2. NQT and induction tutor discuss the school behaviour policy and how to implement it. NQT agrees which behaviour strategies are to be implemented immediately 3. NQT implements the behaviour strategies agreed 4. Induction tutor arranges for head of department to observe lesson and identify any teaching and learning issues hindering good behaviour 5. NQT and head of department discuss the lessons observed. Appropriate teaching and learning strategies discussed. Exemplar lesson plans explained to NQT. NQT agrees a way forward re planning 6. NQT implements the teaching and learning strategies discussed with head of department 7. NQT reads appropriate professional texts on teaching and learning strategies 8. Induction tutor arranges for phase coordinator to observe lessons and focus on teaching and learning 9. NQT reads the individual education plans of pupils with behaviour difficulties in their classes and notes issues and areas which need further guidance 10. NQT and SENCO discuss the individual education plans and how these can be implemented 11. NQT implements the behaviour strategies suggested by the SENCO and evaluates the impact of these strategies in lessons 12. Induction tutor observes one lesson to focus on NQT's implementation of strategies 13. Induction tutor researches and identifies an appropriate behaviour management/assertive discipline course. Books a place and arranges cover for NQT 14. Induction tutor researches and identifies appropriate behaviour management/ assertive discipline texts to recommend to NQT			

15. NQT attends behaviour management course and identifies behaviour strategies to implement
16. NQT implements additional range of strategies identified on behaviour management course and agreed with tutor
17. Induction tutor observes a lesson to focus on NQT's implementation of behaviour strategies from course
18. Induction tutor arranges for NQT to observe with the induction tutor at least two other teachers teaching the pupils who pose most difficulty for NQT
19. NQT implements additional behaviour strategies identified from joint lesson observations with tutor
20. NQT has in-class coaching using earpiece for the NQT and microphone by the tutor
21. NQT given a critical friend/buddy (a second year teacher) for support
22. NQT evaluates, as an ongoing process, the effectiveness of strategies with different groups

Identifying and analysing needs can be time-consuming but – as with any in-depth look at pupils' learning needs – the effort is worthwhile. The next challenge is to find the best way to meet the identified needs, which is the subject of the next chapter.

CHAPTER 6

Professional development

- The range of professional development activities

- Coaching and mentoring

- Observation

- Teachers TV

- Learning conversations – the *TES* website community

- Courses and conferences

- Recognition for your learning

Becoming a better teacher doesn't just happen through trial and error in the classroom. Professional development speeds up the process if it's planned well so that it has a positive impact and gives good value for the time and money that your school invests in it. Having two or three hours a week for professional development is probably the best bit of all your induction entitlement. You'll never have as much opportunity again, so you need to make the most of it, as Julian's Term 1 induction programme shows (Table 2.8). Some new teachers fritter it away in catching up with whatever else needs doing – planning, marking, phone calls – but regret it when they no longer have that time.

> *I've only been on one course and want to participate in as many as possible next term. Any suggestions as to where to look, good websites etc.?* (NQT, Term 2)

I hear this type of comment so often! People often only think of professional development as referring to courses, yet the range of on-the-job, off-the-job, and close-to-the-job professional development opportunities is huge. Rather than wondering what courses to go on, the NQT should approach it from the opposite angle. What does he want to be better at or know more about – and what's the best use of time and money? Budgets are never big enough, if they exist at all. The costs of going on a course, for instance, include the fees, travel, subsistence and supply cover. But there are invisible costs too: the time and effort taken to analyse needs, find the right course, and to book it. Then there's the cost of disruption to pupils' education, and to colleagues who have their timetable altered or who have to support the supply teacher. Against these questions of cost, however, how can the benefits be measured? How do you measure what you've learned; your greater self-confidence and esteem; that new-found energy; what you do differently and its impact on the school and all present and future pupils? It's very hard but these are issues to be aware of.

The range of professional development activities

Once you've decided what you want and need to develop (which isn't easy, as we saw in the previous chapter), choose the best way to do so, bearing in mind how you learn, how much time you have and what resources (human, financial and physical) are available. The TDA (2007c) breaks down sources of CPD into those that come from:

- within school, e.g. coaching/mentoring, lesson observation and feedback, collaborative planning and teaching;

- cross-school networks;

- other external expertise, e.g. external courses or advice offered by, for example, local authorities, universities, subject associations and private providers.

However, there are also further broad categories such as private study. Perhaps one of the most individualised, cheap and flexible ways to get better at teaching is through reading. And it's a lovely thing to do whether you're standing on the train going to work, sitting in the garden, lying on the sofa or even snuggled under the duvet! You can get more knowledge, ideas, food for thought and inspiration.

Here's a list of ways you could develop:

1. Reflect – take some time to think.

2. Ask your pupils – even seven-year-olds will be pretty expert at what teachers do that helps or hinders because they will already have encountered several teachers.

3. Watch someone teach – a teacher, an assistant, a football coach, a learning mentor, anyone.

4. Watch some individuals learning.

5. Discuss things with other new teachers and more knowledgeable others.

6. Try things out.

7. Arrange to visit an 'expert', or ask one in.

8. Go on a course or conference.

9. Watch Teachers TV.

10. Visit another school, similar to or different from yours.

11. Read a book or document.

12. Search the Internet.

13. Find someone to coach-mentor you.

14. Ask someone to observe you.

15. Do a search on the TES staffroom or post your query.

16. Keep a learning log, reflective diary or blog.

17. Arrange for an AST to work with you.

18. Read books and the educational press.

19. Do some research, perhaps with others.

20. Join a network where there is some input, lots of stimulation from people in other schools and an expectation of improving something specific such as provision for gifted and talented pupils.

Activity 6.1 Analysing the professional development involved in one objective

After discussion with her induction tutor, Hannah Piper set herself an objective about teaching mathematical problem-solving better. She observed the head of maths teaching a problem-solving lesson, and they discussed strategies.

'She introduced me to a few handy schemes and books which I've started using and as I've become more confident I've started adapting their ideas and getting feedback from the children. Her recent observation of my teaching of problem-solving made me realise how much progress I'd made – and all the children are doing well, particularly the more able. Would you believe that after a lesson on recording combinations systematically, a girl worked out all the combinations on a bike lock and tried to break into her own bike!' (NQT, Term 3)

Discuss these questions

(a) What elements of professional development led to Hannah's improved teaching of problem-solving?

(b) What lessons can you learn from this?

Coaching and mentoring

I would actually rather have a conversation with my Y8 tutor group than with most of the teachers in my school. They are incredibly rude and unfriendly. (NQT, Term 2)

Adults learn best when they determine their own focus, through being asked questions and being given time to reflect (Bubb and Earley, 2007), so being coached or mentored is an important part of induction. Those acting in the role of coach-mentor – usually induction tutors – need to have the appropriate personal qualities (unlike the teachers referred to above) and the knowledge and skills to be able to coach in subtle but effective ways: by active listening, asking questions and holding new teachers accountable for the actions agreed. Coaching courses often base themselves around either the STRIDE model:

Strengths

Target

Reality

Ideas

Decisions

Evaluations

or the GROW model:

Goals – what do you want?

Reality – what is happening now?

Options – what could you do?

Will – what will you do?

There is a lot of evidence to suggest that acting as a mentor or coach is highly beneficial:

Learning to be a coach or mentor may be one of the most effective ways of enabling teachers to become good and excellent practitioners; current practice appears to concentrate the opportunity amongst those who have already reached this stage. (Cordingley *et al.*, 2005: 17)

People in a coaching-mentoring role should try to help you think of pragmatic solutions rather than perfect ones. When things are tough, induction tutors should encourage the new teacher to think of the kids who do behave and focus on teaching them.

Working with an expert

New teachers can get help from people with expertise. Many local authorities use their ASTs to coach-mentor in this way. Heather Garrett got some fantastic insights about how autistic children see the world from James Allen, an AST from a special school, and his reading of Mark Haddon's *The Curious Incident of the Dog in the Night-time* (2003). She rethought her handling of the autistic child in her class:

> *I've implemented some strategies such as using a timer to help him structure his work and to help him keep calm by letting him go on the classroom workstation when things get stressful.*

Observation

Observation is a powerful tool for professional development. New teachers learn a great deal from watching others, and research has shown that they find observing and being observed the most useful of all induction activities (Totterdell *et al.*, 2002; Bubb *et al.*, 2002). There is much to observe, such as

- teachers in your school – advanced skills teachers, supply teachers, experienced, inexperienced ... anyone!
- support staff
- teachers in other schools – both those that are similar to and different from yours
- someone teaching your class
- someone teaching a lesson that you have planned
- a colleague taking an assembly
- a visiting expert
- a sports coach, an artist or a musician
- a lesson through a child's eyes
- classrooms and corridors.

When you're observing you can:

- watch and understand the development of complex classroom interactions;
- observe in a structured way how, when and with what effect a teacher uses different strategies;
- investigate the different effects of a range of teaching styles and strategies on how pupils respond and learn;

- internalise new approaches you may see in others' practice so that they become part of your repertoire;

- connect knowledge and practice. (GTCE, 2006a: 2)

Good teachers make the most of any opportunities to observe others, formally or informally, around the school. It's very cheering to see that everyone has similar problems, and fascinating to study the different ways people manage them. Steven Heming, who teaches Year 3 at Herbert Morrison Primary School, bravely confessed to being unsure how to teach phonics, so his induction tutor arranged for him to observe her Year 4 class and other staff teaching the word-level section of literacy lessons. He was delighted, saying:

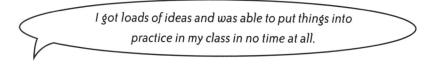

I got loads of ideas and was able to put things into practice in my class in no time at all.

However, observing so that one gets something out of it is not easy. People need to have a focus for observation because there is so much to see that they can end up getting overwhelmed. For instance, someone who wants to improve pace in introductions needs to notice the speed of the exposition, how many pupils answer questions and how the teacher manages to move them on, how instructions are given, how resources are distributed, and how off-task behaviour is dealt with. And then they must think how they could integrate it into their own practice.

There are lots of people you could observe but you need to think who's going to be most useful. Diana had problems with behaviour management, so she was sent to watch a teacher with a good reputation for control. She gained some ideas, but found that much of this experienced teacher's control was 'invisible' – he just cleared his throat and the class became quiet. This did nothing for her self-confidence, in fact she felt worse. After talking things through with her induction tutor, she observed a supply teacher and someone with only a little more experience than herself. These lessons, though not so perfectly controlled, gave Diana much more to think about and she learned lots of useful strategies. Both teachers found it useful to have Diana's views on the lesson, as a non-threatening observer, so they too gained from the experience.

There's much to be said for peer observation – new teachers observing each other for mutual benefit:

While watching exemplar teachers gives you great techniques that you strive to emulate, watching inexperienced teachers shows you much more effectively why certain things that you are doing aren't working much better than a feedback report does.
(NQT, Term 2)

The benefits of being observed include the chance to:

- unpack the complexity of what you do in the classroom so that you can develop and pass it on;

- look closely into one particular aspect of your teaching (such as questioning techniques);

- experiment with new teaching strategies;

- focus on what is happening to the learning of a particular group of pupils;

- discuss your teaching style(s) in a non-judgemental environment;

- connect knowledge and practice. (GTCE, 2006a: 3)

But unless it's set up properly it risks being too cosy, perpetuating the status quo and even mediocrity. There's potential for offence, upset and damaged relationships, so you need training in peer observation techniques and protocol. As one new teacher said: 'Filling in an observation feedback sheet on your friend is scary. There's such a responsibility to get it right.' Egos are fragile. Everyone needs to buy into the principle of peer observation equally and trust each other. You need to know that your peer isn't going to go badmouthing you in the staffroom. But when it works, it's great:

> *I was told a few times that I needed to give my lessons more pace – which I fully accepted – but I wasn't able really to work out how do this, or which parts of my lessons weren't pacy enough. It was only when I saw an NQT in my own subject teach a lesson that I got what they meant about pace because she was too slow too.*
> (NQT, Term 1)

Roy Watson-Davis, an AST at Blackfen School in Bexley, sets up 'learning threes' where NQTs are teamed up across subjects. They help plan each other's lessons, then each teaches a lesson for the other two to observe and then all three discuss what happened.

Three newly qualified teachers at Telferscot Primary in Balham have been encouraged in peer observation by their induction tutor. Behaviour was an issue for all of them, so they decided to focus on that for their observations. When Year 1 teacher, Rebecca Self, was observed she made an effort to use as many strategies for behaviour as she could, not only to help her friends but to prove to herself what she could do. Nursery teacher, Becky Willson, was reassured that she was doing well because there were so many similarities between their teaching. She found that she was able to learn more because everything was more relaxed than in an official observation. Because Becky and Rebecca casually pointed out how Lucy Stewart, who teaches Year 3, overused the word 'excellent', she's now varying how she praises. The conversations after the observation are where the real learning happens.

Feedback on teaching is really valuable – if it's done well (see the next chapter). While on induction you should be observed every six weeks or so, so it's worth getting as much as you can out of it. Teaching requires a lot of self-confidence, so you should be looking to people to boost yours rather than knocking it. With a bit of luck, you'll feel brave enough as the year goes on to be observed teaching something that normally doesn't go well. Being nervous is perfectly normal, but try to address your worries and do something about them, as illustrated in Table 6.1.

Table 6.1: Concerns about being observed

Your concern	Possible solutions
Pupils will be passive – won't engage	Plan something to get them lively. Use talk partners ('turn to your neighbour and tell them the answer to my question').
The behaviour of one child will ruin everything	Plan for an assistant to be with the child. Make sure the work is just right. Or send them to someone else during the observation.
I can't get or keep attention	Do your best but see the observation as a way to get ideas so that you improve.
The pupils play up when I'm observed	Tell them that *they* are being observed. Remind them that you are expecting exemplary behaviour.
Technology will go wrong	Set it up beforehand; check and double-check; have a back-up in case it does go wrong.
I'll forget or lose key resources	Make a list of what you need, tick items off when collected, organise them.
The teaching assistant won't turn up	Keep reminding them that you're relying on them and give them a plan of what they should do.
The pupils will finish work too early	Have some extension work; make the task harder or open-ended.
I'll forget what I planned to do	Do a clear, written plan (that very act helps lodge it in your mind); keep your plan to hand on a distinctive clipboard to avoid it getting lost; have a spare just in case you leave it somewhere; use prompt cards; rehearse the lesson structure in your mind.
I'll forget what to say	Script key parts of the lesson especially questions; rehearse out loud and in your head.
I'll let the class wander off the point	Stay focused; put timings on your plan; write up the learning objective; plan questions that will guide the pupils' thinking.

Here are some suggestions for how to prepare for an observation:

- Plan with even more care than usual. Be completely prepared.

- Have a copy of the lesson plan for the observer.

- Be absolutely clear about what you want the pupils to learn and do.

- Make sure your teaching and the activities match the objectives.

- Have as much stuff as you can written up on the board beforehand.

- Think about what the person observing you is looking for. Address things that haven't gone well before.

- Do everything you can to feel confident – wear your favourite teaching clothes; encourage others to boost you; sleep well; tell yourself that you're going to teach well.

Don't panic if things start to go wrong. Think on your feet. Most teachers have some lessons that go swimmingly, others that are OK and the occasional disasters. There is a huge number of factors to do with you and what you're teaching and then a whole heap to do with different classes, what lesson they've just had, and what time of day it is. So, don't beat yourself up about it.

The dialogue that takes place after a lesson observation is vital, and there's more on this in Chapter 8. There's no such thing as a perfect teacher (except in your mind) so lessons don't have to be perfect, but you can show that you're reflective, making progress and acting on advice. It's bad enough when a lesson doesn't go well but when someone has been in the room observing the chaos, you can sink to new levels of humiliation. Shedding tears in the staff loos is a perfectly normal reaction, but dry your eyes and see the feedback session as a way to get help. That's what induction is all about. Teaching is tough. People aren't born as super-teachers. Everyone has to work at it.

Teachers TV

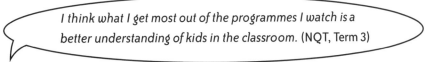

I think what I get most out of the programmes I watch is a better understanding of kids in the classroom. (NQT, Term 3)

Teachers TV can be a great way to help teachers develop. It's on 24 hours a day on digital platforms, but many people find it easier to search for programmes online at www.teachers.tv. You can download them too. Most programmes last only 15 minutes and cover a whole array of topics organised into:

A. Training and professional development
1. Classroom-based CPD: observation, analysis, advice and tips
2. Role-based CPD: support and advice for management, NQTs, teaching assistants, etc.
3. School improvement

B. News and issues
4. News and current affairs
5. Educational issues: information and discussion
6. Career guidance and work–life balance

C. Resources
7. Resource reviews
8. Pupil programmes
9. External resources: visits and working with institutions outside school.

There are many programmes pitched at new teachers, such as those in Table 6.2. If you watch ones like *Practical Tips 1 & 2*, *Working with Others* and *From One Thing to Another*, you'll see me – but remember that the camera adds pounds! Programmes like those in the *Teaching with Bayley* series are great for both new teachers and those who mentor them because John Bayley uses superb coaching skills. Take a look at *Ecoutez* or *Too Much Talk*.

Table 6.2: Programmes specifically for new teachers on Teachers TV

Secondary NQTs	Primary NQTs
Expert Advice 1 and 2	Working with Others
Teaching with Style	Fit to Teach – D-Stressing
Extending Your Range	Fit to Teach – Food and Fitness
Making PPA Work for You	Assessment and Lesson Observation
Survival Secrets	Testing Times
Differentiation	Practical Tips 1 and 2
Reporting to Parents	From One Thing to Another
Sharing the Load	Getting There
Lesson Observation	Managing Behaviour
Time Management	Lesson Planning on the Web
First Year and Beyond	Early Days
Classroom Management	Work/Life Balance
Classroom Encounters with Cowley	Simrit and Victoria – Episodes 1 and 2
Lesson Planning	Passing Out

A primary science programme inspired Cathy Goodey, a teacher at Princes Plain Primary in Bromley:

> I've taught electricity a couple of times with children running round a 'circuit' of other children, mimicking the particle flow. The one on Teachers TV did it similarly but with balls being passed round. If my class could cope with the physical process of continuous passing, each child having one ball at any one time, it'd help their understanding. I'm going to try it out – but now I think about it, with an improved model for the switch!

See how the programmes reassure but spark new ideas? Mrs Goodey says:

> It's reassuring to see methods I've used in the classroom applauded and seeing strategies that are new to me – or ones that I'd simply forgotten.

Teaching can be a solitary business, but Teachers TV gives a window on the world of teaching and learning. You can spy on and discuss lessons without having to intrude or disrupt, and you can dismiss, damn or copy the ideas – and it's all safe.

A NQT course about teaching pupils who speak English as an additional language helped Muinat Daranijoh from Iqra Independent School in Brixton to re-evaluate her practice. After the training, she watched the Teachers TV programmes that were mentioned and found them invaluable in planning for and meeting the needs of pupils.

> *For instance, I sometimes encourage a girl to write in her first language and use this to assess her understanding of concepts. As an extension she sometimes tries to translate her own work in oral English – the rest of the group really find it fascinating.*

Activity 6.2

Learning from a Teachers TV programme

This idea, due to Kevan Bleach of Sneyd School, is useful for both NQTs and/or induction tutors.

Watch *Secondary NQTs – Lesson Planning* (www.teachers.tv/video/1514). This charts modern foreign language teacher Clare Hewitt's progress over her first term of teaching and takes a detailed look at how she is tackling her lesson planning. Clare's finding it hard to motivate Key Stage 4 classes and wants to plan dynamic lessons to keep them interested. Using mind-mapping – a non-linear way of planning – mentor Sarah Williams helps Clare to plan a Year 10 French lesson for pupils of mixed ability.

Use the prompts in Table 6.3 to stimulate discussion and aid your learning.

Table 6.3: Using a Teachers TV programme to stimulate discussion and learning (Bleach, 2006)

Parts of the programme www.teachers.tv/video/1514	Think about...
Lesson planning	■ How should NQTs get on top of planning? ■ What advice should a mentor be offering?
Clare says she's going to use different techniques to appeal to different kinds of learners	■ What does this tell us about Clare's approach to teaching? ■ Should all teachers be thinking about this?
The role of the mentor	■ What is this mentor doing that is useful? ■ What do you expect from the NQT– mentor relationship?
Mind-mapping	■ Is this a useful technique for lesson planning? ■ Are there other techniques you would recommend NQTs try?
The lesson plan	■ How does the plan look? ■ Are there other things she should have included?
The lesson	■ What did you notice here of interest? ■ What did you think of the activities? ■ Anything about her manner or body language? ■ How does she relate to pupils? ■ Any tips here?
Mentor in the lesson	■ How is the mentor observing the lesson?
Feedback session	■ What sort of feedback does a NQT need in the early stages of teaching?
General comments	■ What have you noticed in general about Clare and how she's organising things? ■ What can you learn from this? ■ Any other suggestions?

Learning conversations – the TES website community

All teachers can think of a conversation that has changed their professional practice. The GTC spring 2004 survey of more than 4,000 teachers shows that a substantial majority gain their inspiration for their most effective lessons from talking with colleagues (National Foundation for Educational Research, 2004). If you're looking for learning conversations, support and professional development, the TES website's hugely popular staffroom is freely available 24/7 and 365 days a year. Peecee's feelings are typical:

> *I've found empathy, humour, debates, great websites, camaraderie, and satisfaction in knowing I'm not the only one that crazy stupid things happen to. I've shared oodles of resources and gained oodles as well. I have to admit, I'm addicted.*

Although the TES community is massive it feels cosy, as if you're listening to real friends. Anyone can pop in and an astonishing 130,000 people do so each week, viewing 2.3 million pages. Lots of them just read: 'even though I don't post here very often, I read most nights'. To post a message you join the 268,500 people who've registered. There are between 5,000 and 7,000 postings a day, with over 600 an hour at the peak times between 4 and 5 p.m. and from 7 p.m. to midnight. Bill Hicks, who set up the staffroom, is justly proud: 'After five years of struggle, the forums are now an indispensable part of the fabric of UK education'.

Registering is easy – the hardest part is choosing a witty username that hides your true identity. Some of the site's success must be down to the freedom that comes with this anonymity: people can ask the questions that they'd be too embarrassed to raise elsewhere. Some parts of the staffroom have 'experts' popping in to give advice. I led the way with the newly qualified teacher forum, Selwyn Ward advises teachers panicked by the imminence of inspection, and Oriel looks after the graduate and overseas teacher programme section.

There are over 50 virtual corners of England's staffroom where people with the same interests hang out. Scotland and Wales have their own patches. As well as different forums for 19 subjects, there's a place for every type of school staff – not just teachers but trainees, admin, teaching assistants and governors as well. Bill Hicks reckons:

> *They're one of the few places where teachers and support staff can say what they need to say about their own jobs and the world beyond, where anyone in education with a problem can seek and usually find help from their peers or from experts, and where anyone with an educational axe to grind can get their 15 seconds of fame.*

Schools can be lonely places where people don't have time to have professional learning conversations or share fantastic resources. But the posters on the forum are the very opposite. Want some ideas for tomorrow's lesson? Ask and you'll get ten top tips in no time, as well as worksheets and links to websites. Fiona Duncan, of Longdean School in Hemel Hempstead, describes it as a real learning community, 'a kind of multi-coloured swap shop of ideas and resources'. This has become formalised in the new TES Resource Bank, an area where people can share materials and recommend resources and web pages. In its first year more than 72,000 items were downloaded, like the calendar template that was downloaded by 2,000 people.

Ronan Dunne is one of the many regulars giving so generously of resources and advice that he's seen as one of the saints of the staffroom. A self-confessed addict, he loves it:

> I've spoken to literally thousands of people by e-mail and getting on for a hundred on the phone. This has broadened my horizons, educated me, challenged me, stretched me, and given me a window into hundreds of other schools.

It's often said that the best thing about going on courses is meeting other people, and nowhere is this social side seen more than in the busiest parts of the staffroom, Opinion and Personal. Here you can have a chat, put the world to rights, do some verbal sparring and play games – all without having to leave the house. Many friendships and romances have blossomed in this way – and some marriages. You can't say that about many courses!

Courses and conferences

When well chosen, going on a course is one of the ways to gain a good level of professional development very quickly. There are hundreds of courses run by local authorities, subject associations, national bodies, teacher associations and unions, universities, private outfits and schools themselves. Conferences offer the chance to hear an inspirational speaker and meet up with other people with the same interest. They're a good way to keep informed of the latest developments in the field.

It's ideal for all the NQTs in a school, network or local authority to get together. Some schools, such as Sneyd in Walsall, have a programme of training sessions for new teachers about common concerns which can be addressed *en masse*, but, even more importantly, they benefit from the opportunity to chat. Many local authorities run courses for new teachers. My course for primary NQTs in Lambeth is on 12 half days over the year. These sessions not only give people practical ideas that they can try out straight away, but they're an essential support network for teachers working in one of the most difficult areas in England. New teachers are their own best support network: it's good to realise that they're not the only ones who can't get their class to assembly or who aren't enjoying the job or liking all their pupils. As one said:

> It's lovely when you speak to other reception teachers and they say exactly the same things and you think, that's super, because I know it's not just my children, and it's not just me.

Northamptonshire held a conference for people finishing their induction year so that their second year of teaching would get off to a good start. That's a great idea because people can feel very alone after the intensity of the training and induction years. Some courses and conferences are held after school, on Saturdays or in holidays, which means that pupils' learning isn't disrupted. Not many people seem to know that you can get paid to attend courses in your own time – after all, you're saving the school the cost of a supply teacher or the hassle of covering absence internally.

The opportunity to network with other new teachers and broaden horizons is an important factor in deciding where to go on a course. Those organised by the local authority enable you to meet up with people from local schools and get to know the advisers and inspectors, which is hugely advantageous. Sometimes the local scene gets a little insular, so going to a venue that attracts a wider range of people can be great and gives a broader perspective. It's also a good way to find out about jobs!

One of the big advantages of going on a course is that actually being out of the school building and atmosphere gives you some time and space to think, to reflect. However, there's a danger that though you're inspired on the day, you go back into school and by 9.05 you're too overwhelmed to put things into practice. You need to be an active learner, always thinking about what you can implement in your context. A two-and-a-half-hour session for NQTs on managing behaviour with John Bayley in October has had a lasting effect on Hannah Stechman's class at Johanna Primary:

I've changed how I praise: sometimes I'll boost the whole class but at other times I'll speak or give a thumbs up privately to an individual. Techniques like proximal praise are working well for children who always want my attention so rather than tell them off for shouting out I praise someone sitting near them who is doing the right thing.

The class are very noisy so I made a sound chart to show where the noise level needs to be – and is! Speaking from different parts of the room keeps everyone on their toes and aware of what they're meant to be doing. I try to keep my voice at a low pitch – it sounds calmer and more authoritative – and the children have started to speak in the same way! At challenging moments during the day things that John spoke about pop into my head: it's so wonderful to have a range of strategies to draw on.
(NQT, Term 3)

Nicky Jones, from The Livity School in Brixton, picked up some really useful tips and drama games on a course specifically for people who teach children with profound and multiple learning difficulties. But most of all,

I took away a reassuring sense that I'm doing the same as they are and employing similar teaching methods and was really pleased that the other teachers appreciated my ideas. The best kind of professional development possible is learning from each other! (NQT, Term 3)

Some courses that last for more than one day have activities built into them so that people are forced to 'learn, do and review'. For instance, within my four-day accredited induction tutor course, participants are asked to discuss Transition Point 2 with their NQTs, set up an individualised induction programme, set and review objectives and related action plans for the NQTs' development through the year; write feedback from lessons that they have observed; and write assessment reports at the end of each term. All these are tasks that induction tutors have a statutory responsibility to do but being on the course means that people get a chance to discuss them – and be rewarded through gaining 30 credits towards a graduate diploma or master's degree.

Recognition for your learning

Professional development is an entitlement, an expectation and a responsibility for teachers throughout their careers. But it's win–win: not only do you become a better teacher, but also you have evidence that you're meeting standards to help you on your career path. Remember that the core standards require new teachers to 'Evaluate their performance and be committed to improving their practice through appropriate professional development', and by the time you're ready to cross the threshold onto the upper pay scale you have to 'Contribute to the professional development of colleagues through coaching and mentoring, demonstrating effective practice, and providing advice and feedback' (TDA, 2007b).

Helping other teachers

> *When I'm snowed under, it's nice to be able to help someone else. It's a bit of a confidence boost when you can give a useful answer! (NQT)*

In schools, there's always someone who knows the answer to a question about the curriculum but remember that you're not a know-nothing new bug, because there are lots of things you know and can do through being fresh from training that are useful to experienced colleagues and other new teachers. Michael Tidd, a new teacher in a middle school in West Sussex, is a shining example. He says:

> *While I have to learn a great deal from others, I can also be useful in helping people and this has helped me really feel part of the team. I suppose lots of people go into teaching because they want to make a difference, and it's nice to know that sometimes I can be leading that difference-making, not just following someone else.*

Thinking more about a subject in order to help someone sort out a problem sharpens your understanding. Regular poster on the TES NQT forum, trinity0097, says:

> *I don't see the point of sitting on knowledge that others want and not sharing. I get a bit of a warm fuzzy feeling when someone asks something of me in particular because I'm known to have a strength in that subject or area.*

And of course, there are few people more grateful for help or support than busy teachers.

But both NQTs and induction tutors can get recognition from elsewhere. The GTC Teacher Learning Academy (TLA) offers professional recognition for teachers' learning through development work in school. TLA professional recognition is achieved by addressing each of six core dimensions:

1. Engagement with a knowledge base

2. Assessing peer and coaching support

3. Planning a change activity

4. Carrying out the activity

5. Evaluating

6. Disseminating.

You can work on projects individually or collaboratively, in your own school or across institutions. Verification of the quality for acceptance within the TLA is carried out by other teachers, who have been trained to do this. The TLA is independent of any university, but the scheme has been developed so that university accreditation is an option for teachers who make successful submissions at Stages 2 or 3. For more information go to www.gtce.org.uk.

With many PGCEs now carrying master's level credits, consider enrolling on an MA course. Some courses, like the Master of Teaching at the Institute of Education in London, are geared towards new teachers. It's great intellectual stimulation. Most MAs will require you to do some action research in school, which has numerous spin-offs. One teacher uses talk partners as a way of developing the learning of all pupils, especially the large number who speak English as an additional language, but she is investigating what types of pairing work best:

■ Single-sex pairs

■ Boy-girl pairs

■ Ability pairs

■ Friendship pairs

■ Does it differ with the age of the children?

Your learning can be used for evidence of professional reflection for Chartered London Teacher status so long as they cover one of the 12 CLT standards, make a difference in school and are disseminated as widely as possible to maximise the benefit (DfES, 2007). In the next chapter we look at how observations of new teachers are a valuable form of professional development as well as a significant way to monitor development.

CHAPTER 7

Observation

- The benefits of observation

- The rules

- Be aware of issues

- Bad practice

- Good practice in setting up an observation

- During the observation

- After the lesson

This chapter is intended for people who support new teachers – mentors, induction tutors, senior staff and appropriate bodies.

The benefits of observation

Observation is a powerful tool for assessing and monitoring a teacher's progress. In a large-scale research project (Totterdell *et al.*, 2002; Bubb *et al.*, 2002) 89 per cent of NQTs said that they found being observed really useful: it was rated the most useful of all professional development activities, alongside observing other teachers. Observation has enormous benefits, as a way not only to monitor and assess but also to support new teachers. Done well, it should provide an invaluable context for teachers to reflect upon and discuss in detail the teaching and learning that happen in their class. It should be an opportunity to have strengths and successes recognised, problems accurately diagnosed and areas for development identified. The benefits for the observer are also considerable. You learn so much from seeing other people's practice, and can't help but reflect on your own practice and pedagogy.

The rules

> *I was given this job without being observed and have had no observations at all. In some ways this is less pressure but in others it is more – I feel like I need some feedback to improve. I haven't a clue if what I'm doing is right or wrong!* (NQT, start of Term 3)

Being clear about what the induction guidance has to say – and what it doesn't say – about observation is essential.

> The NQT's teaching should be observed during their first four weeks in post, and thereafter at least once in any six to eight week period, e.g. once each half term. Where the NQT works part-time, the intervals between observations should be adjusted accordingly, but the first observation should take place in the first half term. (DfES, 2003a: para. 72)

Many people think that observing their new teachers early on is cruel, but I think that leaving them too long without any feedback on how they're doing is more cruel and dangerous. Look at things from a new teacher's point of view: they've been used to teaching with a 'real' teacher around and have normally had formal feedback every week. Now that they're flying solo they're desperate to get reassurance that they're doing OK and to be helped. Many problems encountered at the start are to do with organisation: seating arrangements, pencils or other resources. These are things that are easy for an experienced teacher to spot and to help the new teacher remedy, but the longer things are left, the harder they are to diagnose and to deal with. In no time at all minor problems with organisation can turn into major discipline problems. It's like gardening: life is so much easier if you pull out weeds from the root as soon as you spot them, but if they overrun a flower bed you've got a battle on your hands!

The national research on induction found that over a quarter of NQTs weren't observed during their first four weeks (Totterdell *et al.*, 2002). The reasons for this were as follows:

- There were too many other things to do at the beginning of the school year.

- Induction tutors thought that NQTs needed time to settle before being observed. (I think this was often misplaced kindness.)

- Induction tutors didn't know that they should do an early observation and hadn't been trained to do so.

It's a good idea to get a date in the diary for the observation early on and build this into your induction policy and programme.

New teachers should have at least six observations throughout the year, spaced out at roughly six-week intervals. You would think it's common sense not to observe right at the end of term, but I have known it to happen. There is no guidance on the maximum number of observations; in many ways the more the better, so long as they're done well and are helping the new teacher to improve.

Think about what else the induction guidance doesn't say: for instance, it says nothing about how long NQTs should be observed for. You don't have to do a whole lesson. In fact I'm sure you'll have plenty of things to say after watching for only about 20 minutes but it depends on what your focus is. If somebody has been trying to improve the ends of lessons, including tidying up, packing away and leaving the room in an orderly fashion, then it makes sense to observe one or two ends of lessons, which could just take five minutes. Here is what the guidance says:

> Observations should focus on particular aspects of the NQT's teaching which are agreed in advance between the NQT and the observer. The choice of focus for the observations should be informed by (i) the requirements for the satisfactory completion of induction and (ii) the NQT's objectives for career development. (DfES, 2003a: para. 72)

There are no rules about how much notice observers should give, although it's clear that there should be some in order to agree a focus. Note also that the focus should relate to the core standards, which are different from the criteria for inspection that so many schools like to use when they observe.

A variety of people can observe NQTs teach and, although it's desirable, headteachers don't have to observe a new teacher unless they're struggling:

> Where the induction tutor is not the head teacher, the head should observe the teaching of any NQT considered not to be making satisfactory progress, and review the available evidence. Where the induction tutor is the head teacher, the head should ensure that a third party reviews the evidence and observes the NQT. (DfES, 2003a: para. 115)

The discussion after the lesson is going to be the most valuable part of the whole process and the guidance is clear that there should be verbal and written feedback:

> The NQT and the observer should have a follow-up discussion to analyse lessons observed. Arrangements for follow up discussions to observations should be made in advance and a brief written record should be made on each occasion. This record should relate to the NQT's objectives for development and indicate where action should be taken. It should show any revision of objectives. (DfES, 2003a: para. 74)

Be aware of issues

As induction tutor you not only have to carry out observations but also coordinate other people to do them, which can be tricky. Across all schools there's more observation of teaching than ever before, carried out for a range of reasons and by a range of people – inspectors, headteachers, members of senior leadership teams, subject leaders, induction tutors, mentors, teacher tutors and governors. With the short-notice inspection system, senior staff are watching lessons so often and so negatively that some say it's damaging teachers' morale and confidence. It shouldn't be like that.

Observation needs to be done well so that it is helpful to teachers and benefits pupils. But the value of an observation depends on how well it is planned, executed and discussed afterwards –

I think there should be a firm structure to follow when observing lessons and clearer standards for the NQTs to meet because at times some mentors have their own agendas and standards by which they assess the NQT whether they mean to or not and these may not be fair or appropriate. (NQT, Term 2)

and that depends on how knowledgeable and astute the observer is and how open the new teacher is to using this as an opportunity to develop. Yet few people have had any in-depth training in how to observe or even to discuss what effective teaching and learning is. Both are crucial if observers are to feel secure in their judgements and the observed to feel that it is a valid exercise. So you may want to arrange some professional development in this area for yourself and colleagues. It's helpful to get some feedback on how beneficial your own and colleagues' observations have been. Do ask whether they're useful!

Remember that observation takes time (and thus money) because for any hour you spend watching a lesson you should allocate about 3 hours:

- 30 minutes to plan it with the teacher and prepare for it;

- 1 hour to observe and make notes;

- 1 hour to reflect and write up a summary;

- 30 minutes for the post-observation discussion.

Do you like being observed? It's almost always a stressful experience, not only for the teacher but also for the observer, so recognise feelings. Teachers feel a pressure for observations to go well and want them to be conducted fairly. You may find observing stressful, because you feel inexperienced and uncertain of the best way to go about it. The year group and area of the curriculum to be taught may not be familiar. Do you worry that the quality of your observation and feedback will compare unfavourably with that of others? You've got to move new teachers forward while maintaining a good relationship, and this can lead to misplaced kindness. Some new teachers complain that they aren't sufficiently challenged, and that the observation and feedback are only superficial. This is particularly true of the most successful teachers, but, like our most able pupils, they too need to be helped to develop professionally.

Think about the context of the observation: the stage the new teacher is at; how they're feeling; their previous experiences of being observed; your relationship; the time in the school year, week and day; and the disposition of the class. Be aware that your presence in the room, however unobtrusive, will have some influence on what happens in the room – pupils may behave better or worse, which can be a challenge to your authority. Certainly the teacher may be more inhibited than usual. No lesson is typical and certainly it's worth bearing in mind that, as Hal Portner, (2002: 45) says, 'When you observe a class, you actually observe a class being observed'. To build up trust, arrange for the teacher to observe you before you watch them.

It's also valuable to recognise your own values, beliefs and moods. When I was less experienced I had strong views on what I considered good teaching to be. With hindsight, this was very subjective, narrow and arrogant. This is why it is important to concentrate on the progress the pupils make before judging the effectiveness of the teaching – and to avoid preconceptions about the teacher. The more I observe other people, the more convinced I am that there is no one best way to teach.

Bad practice

Bad practice in observing causes great problems and can damage teachers' confidence. I've heard of situations where the observer:

- arrived late and disrupted the lesson

- observed without any notice

- intervened

- corrected the teacher's errors in front of pupils

- looked bored or disapproving – or fell asleep!

- let their mobile ring – and answered it!

- did not give any feedback

- nitpicked over inconsequential things

- gave written feedback without an opportunity for discussion

- contradicted the views of previous observers

- felt that they had to criticise a fantastic lesson

- gave simplistic feedback without any ideas for further development

- made erroneous judgements based on poor knowledge of the context

- upset the teacher without giving positive ways forward.

Teachers undergoing statutory induction should be judged on progress towards meeting the core standards but obviously if they're inspected, the Ofsted framework will be used. Because Ofsted strikes fear into many people's hearts, some induction tutors and headteachers like to pretend they're inspectors and grade lessons. There's no law against this ... except common sense. Inspectors inspect, but induction is about being supported and monitored – and thereby moved on to develop into a better teacher. I don't think people should go around grading because it's unhelpful, unnecessary and may even be inaccurate: are you a trained inspector? I am (well, I gave it up some years ago after inspecting about 25 schools) but I still find grading hard especially when it could be a high satisfactory (3) or low good (2). And who likes being told that they're satisfactory?

It's not fair that she should be so upset. With the inspection criteria the relationship between

> *I was observed under Ofsted criteria and heavily criticised with hardly any positive comments. Got a satisfactory – just. I was a good/excellent student during training and am really upset.* (NQT, Term 1)

teaching and the pupils' learning is all important. Mandi, a new teacher, was upset: 'I got an unsatisfactory rating on my first observation (22 September)'. She was told her lesson was unsatisfactory because a small number of pupils were off task and didn't produce good enough work. It's amazing that at three weeks into her career only a small number of pupils didn't work hard enough! She was worried about the consequences of getting the 'unsatisfactory' rating, when the only impact of this should have been that the school gave more targeted support to enable her to succeed.

This sort of experience will knock any teacher's confidence, which is a crazy thing to do – nobody can teach without heaps of it. It's much better for the observer to talk about strengths, successes, small improvements and areas for development. Obviously there are going to be many things new teachers could improve but there should be discussion about what to prioritise.

Some schools see trainees and NQTs as guinea pigs to practise their observation and feedback

> *Rarely a week goes past without someone coming in to watch me, requiring detailed lesson planning and a one-hour meeting after school to feed back.* (NQT, Term 2)

skills on, which really isn't fair. It can be really damaging to have your every move analysed. Some people have been over-observed and that has put them under lots of pressure. One NQT was observed 12 times in nine weeks and said 'I feel like I'm in goldfish bowl'. Three people watched him at the same time on one occasion – the head, deputy and a consultant who was also an inspector. Stressful or what!

As with many areas, it is useful to have a policy on procedures and good practice before, during and after an observation so that there is consistency and clarity. The rest of this chapter will provide some things to think about.

Good practice in setting up an observation

Like so many things in life, preparation is all, so the observer and the NQT need to meet beforehand to:

- set a date and time;
- choose the focus;
- clarify the purpose;
- show the format of written feedback;
- discuss protocols;
- set a time for discussing what has been observed.

Plan when the observation is to take place and how long it will be for. A whole lesson is ideal but is not always necessary, depending on the focus. Around a week's notice seems fair for all concerned. Choose a lesson that the teacher feels happy with and that will give you the information you need. If you want to get a rounded picture of the teacher try to observe a lesson at a time of the day and week that hasn't been covered before. If teachers keep a simple record (such as the one in Table 7.1) of when they've been observed, you can see gaps at a glance. There's so much difference between how one functions in the morning and later in the day! While your diaries are out, agree a time and place to discuss the lesson, giving both of you time to reflect. Ideally, do this at the end of the day or at most within 24 hours of the observation. Give the teacher a written copy of the arrangements.

Table 7.1 Record of lessons observed: Oliver

Date	Time	Class	Subject	Focus	Observer
27 Sept	9.30–10.00	Y3	Literacy	Organisation; relationships	Induction tutor
3 Nov	9.30–10.30	Y3	Literacy	Behaviour and pace	Literacy coordinator
18 Jan	11–12	Y3 low set	Numeracy	Assessment for learning	Induction tutor
2 Mar	11–12	Y3	Science	Questioning; higher-order thinking	Science coordinator
19 May	11–12	Y3	PE	Athletics; control and organisation outside	Headteacher
13 June	1.30–2.30	Y3	Art	Collaboration; creativity	Induction tutor

Agree a focus, which will often be to look at something the teacher is trying to get better at. This won't exclude you from noticing and commenting on other things, but will ensure that you have information on the key area that you are working on. In all cases, it should be linked to the core standards and ultimately helping pupils learn more effectively. Clarify why are you observing – the purpose. Is it for assessment or professional development, or both?

Let teachers have a copy of the pro forma and the criteria you will be judging them by. Also be clear about what will happen to the observation notes you make: will they be given to a third party or not? What happens if you have grave concerns about aspects of the lesson? Will the quality of teaching and learning be graded? It's not necessary and can cause problems, but if it is, then observers should be trained to do this accurately and teachers should be informed.

Discuss ground rules such as how your presence is to be explained to the class, what you are going to do, where you should sit, and your exact time of arrival. Discuss what you will need before or at the beginning of the observation, such as the lesson plan and access to the planning file. If you need something in advance, agree when the teacher is going to give it to you.

Whatever you use should be appropriate to the purpose, context and focus – for example, inspection forms should be used only for inspection! There are ones that require very little writing, because you just tick boxes, but though that makes it easy for the observer it's next to no good for the teacher who will want to know why one box was ticked rather than another. Some people write a running record of what happens in a lesson with a few ideas dotted around like a stream of consciousness – but I guess a video will do that as well.

There are two sorts of writing from an observation: notes you make during the lesson; and a summary of strengths and areas for development for feedback. I think both should be used. That way you can make informal jottings during the lesson, knowing that they'll be summarised in a tidy product.

My personal preference (and it is a personal thing) is for the formats shown in Tables 7.2 and 7.3 (see also Template 2 in the Appendix), which I designed to suit most types of lessons. Let me explain why. When I'm observing I need to concentrate on what's happening rather than trying to answer questions or fill in boxes, so I need a copy of the teacher's lesson plan and a blank piece of paper to write down what seems to me to be important. I don't write too much about the structure of the lesson – I scribble bits on the copy of the lesson plan for this, using ticks, noting down times that certain things happened and making the occasional comment ('nice idea', 'kids fidgeting'). However, there's a danger that I'll only notice what's in my face. That's where the prompts come in: glancing down them reminds me to make a judgement on the quality of the plan, organisation, the teacher's voice or whatever. The prompts cover the features that are in the standards: relationships, communication, etc. That way, even if I don't have time in the lesson to write about these points in detail I'll make a jotting or give it a tick, cross, question mark or exclamation mark and maybe write about them in the summary.

Table 7.2 Classroom observation – in-class jottings

Teacher: Lyndsay	Obs focus: whole class teaching in intros
Observer: Sara Bubb	Class: Y3
Support staff: None in this part of lesson	Subject: English
Date: Tues 9 Feb Start 1.40 end 2.03	Learning obj: Style of fairy tales; devise who, what, where, when, why, how questions – character, event, setting, time, motives, explanation

Prompts	ok	Comments and evidence. What impact does teaching have on pupils?
Relationships	✓	Well done, you're very well prepared for this lesson and have planned it in detail. Well resourced and organised. Clear plan that you implemented well, exploiting opportunities to get children reading and expanding their vocabulary.
Expectations	✓	
School policies	✓	
Communication	✓	Pupils come in calmly and settle down on the carpet sitting in rows – clearly know expected behaviour and have been well trained. Caring attitude shown towards Mark who wasn't feeling too good – he knows just what to do if he feels ill, which is important.
Collaboration	✓	
Subject knowledge	✓	Good voice – clear articulation and not too rushed so that all children could understand you. Did you share the learning objective? It is school policy. I'm not too clear about what you wanted them to learn or why.
Planning	✓	
Objectives	?	Big book well positioned so that all could see it. Good pointing at the words so that all children could read aloud. How many times have they read this version of Cinderella before? Good to ask if there were any words they didn't understand. How else could you have helped the children understand 'spiteful' so that they weren't confused? It's not easy to define - could they have acted it?
T&L strategies	✓	
Behaviour	✓	
Organisation	✓	Other than that you showed confident subject knowledge and made accurate use of technical language such as 'genre' – and you expected pupils to use these terms, which is good.
Resources	✓	

Use of time	✓	Positive feedback & use of praise to boost children's self confidence – as a result many are keen to contribute. Good balance between easy questions and those that
Questioning	✓	require more thought. Were the questions differentiated so that the more able
Motivating	?	were challenged? Without knowing the children it's hard for me to judge.
Differentiation	–	Impressive control – all the above contribute help in this area but you are also very confident yourself and this helps. You expect the children to behave in a certain way
Other adults	?	(i.e. sit in rows on the carpet), and they do!
Assessment	–	Good that you wrote the 'who, what,' etc questions on the flip chart before the lesson, and at a height that all could see. Clear board work.
Plenary	✓	
Learning environment	✓	Time: 1.50 Pupils on task: all Time: 2.00 Pupils on task: all

Table 7.3 Classroom observation – summary

Teacher: Lyndsay	Obs focus: whole class teaching in intros
Observer: Sara Bubb	Class: Y3
Support staff: None in this part of lesson	Subject: Literacy
Date: Tues 9 Feb Start 1.40 end 2.03	Learning obj: style of fairy tales; devise who, what, where, when, why, how questions – character, event, setting, time, motives, explanation

Strengths of the lesson

Well done, Lyndsay, this was a lesson intro that I enjoyed. In particular the strengths were:

✓ Your enjoyment of teaching

✓ Caring attitude to children e.g. Mark who wasn't feeling too good

✓ Strong voice, professional demeanour and self confidence

✓ Clear plan that you implemented well, exploiting opportunities to get children reading and expanding their vocabulary

✓ Confident subject knowledge and use of technical language such as 'genre' – and expecting pupils to use these terms, which they did (brilliant!)

✓ Well resourced and organised

✓ Positive feedback and use of praise to boost children's self confidence – as a result many were keen to contribute

✓ Balance between easy questions and those that required more thought

✓ Impressive control – all the above contribute in this area but you are also very confident yourself and this helps. You expect the children to behave in a certain way (i.e. sit in rows on the carpet), and they do!

✓ Good use of the big book version of Cinderella and flip chart, and at a height that all could see

Areas for further development

1. Improve more pupils' learning in whole class carpet sessions by

■ being clear about what you want them to achieve, and let them know

■ plan for differentiated questions

Teacher's comment

Thanks. This was really helpful and I'm clear about what's going well and what to try to improve.

Signatures: Lyndsay Sara

I use the format in Table 7.2 as a jotting sheet, just for me, knowing that my notes will be pulled together in a tidy summary afterwards. It'll be full of abbreviations, quotations of what was actually said, unfinished statements and awful handwriting and grammar! If the teacher wants to see what I've written that's fine, but the format of Table 7.3 is what I want to share with them. On this sheet I spend time reflecting on what is significant in the lesson, writing the strengths and successes liberally before I see the teacher and thinking about what might be areas for development, as illustrated in Paul's case in Chapter 8. I keep these in my head rather than commit them to paper because it's important for me to know what the teacher thought of the lesson. Some things are easier to approach orally or in an oblique way.

Activity 7.1

Observing a lesson

Get hold of the free Teacher Training Agency pack, *Supporting Assessment for the Award of Qualified Teacher Status: Year 3*, publication no. 96-1/2-00. This came out in 2000 and was issued to support teacher training so there's likely to be a copy in the school. It consists of a video and booklet. Watch primary teacher, Lyndsay, teach a literacy lesson to a Year 3 class and read what I have written about the introduction (Tables 7.2 and 7.3).

During the observation

> Every observation I have, formal or informal, seems to be a list of what I could have done better. Do I just accept that teaching is a profession of continual criticism and very little encouragement? It demotivates me so badly, no one seems to notice it's not actually encouraging me at all. (NQT, Term 2)

Go in with a positive frame of mind: ineffective teaching is rare, so get ready to spot the good stuff! This may sound obvious and patronising but I've known so many teachers who almost automatically look for things to criticise, things that they would have done better. It is essential to look at teaching in relation to learning. One must always be thinking about cause and effect. Why are the pupils behaving as they are? The cause is often related to teaching. Thus, the observer needs to look carefully at what both the teacher and the pupils are doing. Too often the teacher gets most of the attention, yet the product of their work is the pupils' learning – the proof of the pudding.

Be as unobtrusive as possible, but remember Portner's (2003) quote and that your very presence is affecting the lesson. Like a science experiment, your presence in the room is a variable. If the teacher has not given you a place to sit, choose one which is outside the direct line of the teacher's vision, but where you can see the pupils and what the teacher is doing. At the side and half way down is best. When the pupils are doing activities, move around to ascertain the effectiveness of the teacher's explanation, organisation and choice of task. Look at different groups (girls and boys; high, average and low attainers; and pupils with English as an additional language or special needs) to see whether everyone's needs are being met. Ask things like 'Sorry, what did Miss ask you to do?' and 'What are you learning? Why?'

Read the lesson plan, paying particular attention to the learning objective. Is it a sensible objective, and do the pupils understand it? It's useful to annotate the plan, showing what parts went well, when pace slowed, and so forth. Look at the teacher's planning file and pupils' work to see what the lesson is building on.

Make notes about what actually happens (with significant timings), focusing on the agreed areas but keeping your eyes open to everything. Make clear judgements as you gather evidence. Refer to the criteria you agreed to use – have a copy with you. Try to tell 'the story' of the lesson, by noting causes and effects. For instance, what was it about the teacher's delivery that caused pupils' rapt attention or fidgeting? Think about the pupils' learning and what it is about the teaching that is helping or hindering it. Note what pupils actually achieve. Teachers are not always aware that some pupils have managed to write only the date and that others have exceeded expectations.

Avoid teaching the pupils yourself or interfering in any way. This is very tempting! Pupils will often expect you to help them – but once you help one, others will ask. This will distract you from your central purpose, which is to observe the teaching and learning. It is not wise to intervene in controlling the class unless things get out of hand, because it can undermine the teacher's confidence and may confuse the pupils, who will see you as the one in charge rather than their teacher. As far as possible be unobtrusive.

Remember that your presence will normally have an effect on the pupils – if you're an established member of staff they will often be better behaved but occasionally show off. It is sometimes useful to leave the room for a few minutes and loiter nearby to see if the noise level rises when you're not there and to get a feel for the atmosphere as you go back in. This can also be used when the lesson is going badly because it gives the teacher the opportunity to pull the class together.

Look friendly and positive throughout, even (and especially) if things are not going well. Say something positive to the teacher and the children as you leave the class. The teacher will be very anxious, and will almost always think the worst unless reassured. Ideally, give an indication that you were pleased with what you saw but if that's not possible be empathetic – 'you must have the patience of a saint!' or 'fractions are so hard'.

After the lesson

> *When you have an unsatisfactory observation it really knocks your confidence, I have only had one and yet it has made me dread being observed ever since.* (NQT, Term 3)

Even if there's time, don't fall into the trap of discussing the lesson straight away because you need to think about the teaching and learning you have seen, focusing on strengths, what has got better and one or two areas for development. Be clear about your main message – this will take some thinking about. There is no point listing every little thing that could have been better: there always will be something since there's no such thing as a perfect lesson. You need to have 'the big picture' in your mind in order to convey it to the teacher. Remember it should be useful to them, to help them develop. You want to avoid the extremes of crushing them or giving the impression that things are better than they really are. It is a very fine line to tread, so your knowledge of the context and the teacher is essential. In the next chapter we will explore how to discuss teaching following an observation.

Discussing teaching – verbally and in writing

- Some general principles

- Deciding how to approach a discussion

- Framework for a post-lesson observation discussion

- Written feedback

Discussing teaching and learning is vital if people are to develop. I don't like the term 'feedback' as it suggests that the observer is going to do all the talking and the teacher will sit and listen, passively. People develop by thinking and coming to solutions themselves rather than being told what to do and criticised. But think about the physical setting of the discussion. Choose a place where you won't be disturbed – you never know how someone is going to react. Even when the lesson has gone well, teachers can become emotional because, if nothing else, they're very tired! Providing drink and a bite to eat is a nice caring touch and can oil the wheels of your discussion. Position chairs at right angles for the most conducive atmosphere. This enables you to have eye contact but not in the formal direct way that sitting opposite someone across a desk would ensure. Mind you, sometimes you might want to choose such a formal setting to get a tough message across. Sitting next to someone is awkward because it's hard to get eye contact or to move away.

Some general principles

Try to ask questions to guide the teacher's thinking, but not in a way that intimidates or implies criticism. Encourage reflection and listen well by asking open-ended questions, such as:

- How do you think the lesson went?

- What were you most pleased with? Why?

- What were you trying to achieve?

- What did the pupils learn? What did the lower/higher attaining pupils learn?

- Why do you think the lesson went the way it did?

- Why did you choose that activity?

- Were there any surprises?

- When you did –– the pupils reacted by –– Why do you think that happened?

- Help me understand what you took into account when you were planning.

- If you taught that lesson again, what, if anything, would you do differently?

- What will you do in the follow-up lesson?

Avoid talking about yourself or other teachers you have seen, unless this will be useful to the teacher. Comments such as 'I wouldn't have done that' or 'I would have done this' are inappropriate and can irritate and alienate the teacher. It is sometimes tempting to talk about your most awful lesson. This can be comforting for the teacher, but can detract from the purpose of the discussion. Aim for the teacher to do most of the talking and thinking. Paraphrase and summarise what the teacher says. This helps you concentrate on what is being said and is very helpful in getting a clear shared understanding of what the teacher thinks. It involves reflecting back your interpretation of what you have heard, which can be very useful for the teacher. Use phrases such as 'So what you mean is...' or 'In other words...'.

Be aware of your body language and notice the teacher's. A large proportion of communication is non-verbal. Also, watch what you say and how you say it. Focus on the teaching and learning that took place, using specific examples of what pupils said and did. Be positive throughout. Be sensitive to how the teacher is taking your feedback, and ease off if necessary: Rome wasn't built in a day. There will be other opportunities for raising points, perhaps through subtle hints in the staffroom.

Deciding how to approach a discussion

Activity 8.1

Read the observer's notes (Observation 1) about Paul's maths lesson with a Year 3 and 4 middle set. List what you deduce are his strengths, weaknesses and areas for development. How would you tackle issues with him?

Observation 1: Paul's maths lesson

The maths lesson was a new unit on shape. Lesson plan was very detailed and three pages long – almost a script. Well organised and resourced. Paul shared the learning objectives at the start of the lesson but used exactly the words written on the plan, 'to explore, visualise and construct cubes'. He didn't attempt to explain what they meant or what the children would be able to do or understand by the end of the lesson. The children I spoke to didn't understand. The lesson was really an investigation on ways to make nets of cubes to see which way of arranging the squares would work.

Activity 8.1

The lesson started with a test, which did not seem appropriate. Paul asked questions and children individually had to write the answer on a white board and then mark each other's. Some questions were very hard, such as 'What is a nine-sided shape called?' He asked, 'What is a four-sided shape called?' but he was looking for the term 'quadrilateral', rather than 'square' and 'rectangle'. He made no attempt to notice who was getting answers right and who was getting them wrong. A fair number of children found it very hard.

His expectations were high, but perhaps too high. For instance, he started talking about congruent shapes which confused the children and wasn't pertinent to the learning objective. However, other explanations were clear and fairly well scaffolded. He had excellent control and a good level of mutual respect. Questioning was weak. Almost all the questions were closed. He only chose people with their hands up and predominantly chose boys. At one point he asked eight boys and only one girl. His voice dominated the lesson: he missed opportunities to get children explaining ideas. There was no differentiation written on the plan or apparent to me as an observer.

So, there were a great many concerns, but strengths too! Before speaking to the teacher in such a case it's helpful to list strengths and concerns. When you look at the strengths in Table 8.1 you can see that they are really significant and need to be clearly conveyed and celebrated. Of the weaknesses, which do you think are the ones that are most significant or from which other issues could be covered? Choose the biggest hitter – the one that's going to make most difference to all subsequent lessons. Imagine the five weaknesses as roads you could go down. Avoid ones that are culs-de-sac: the ones that Paul will argue with. For instance, he may disagree with you over whether the test was inappropriate or too hard – he knows the children better than you – so that's not the best route to take. Similarly, he could argue that there was differentiation by outcome in the task which was a reasonably open-ended investigation. You're on surer ground with the issue of the learning objective not being clear and not exactly matched to the activity, because you have evidence from the children. It's a good road to go down and one that will have a significant impact on teaching and learning.

Table 8.1 The strengths and weaknesses of Paul's lesson

Strengths	Weaknesses
Very detailed plan	Learning objective not understood by children.
Well organised and resourced	Activity didn't match the learning objective
Explanations clear	Test was inappropriate way to start and made some
Excellent control	children anxious – too hard
Enthusiastic	Questioning
Mutual respect	No differentiation
High expectations	Missed opportunities for learning
Practical – drawing and making nets	

Framework for a post-lesson observation discussion

It's useful to have some sort of structure for the post-lesson observation discussion or professional dialogue – a learning conversation. You need to use time well, feel in control of the situation and know where you want to get. A common feedback structure is shown in Table 8.2. However, the style of this structure – telling someone their strengths and then areas for development – tends towards the teacher being passive, listening to what the observer has to say. The teacher doesn't pay attention to the strengths because they are waiting for the 'but'. This is not always the best way to encourage someone to develop professionally. Your aim should be to encourage the teacher to play a more active part and engage in a dialogue.

Table 8.2 Typical feedback structure (Bubb and Hoare, 2001: 69)

Phase	Commentary
1 Observer asks teacher 'How do you think the lesson went?'	Teacher doesn't know what the observer's judgement is, so may be cagey. Some teachers say little ('It was OK') and others say too much. Some people go off on a tangent that after 10 minutes leaves you utterly confused.
Observer either: 2(a) goes over their notes chronologically with strengths and weaknesses mingled; or 2(b) outlines strengths and then areas to develop	2(a) This gives a detailed picture of the lesson, but overall may not give a clear message about what was good and what needs to be improved. or 2(b) Strengths and areas for development are clear, but the teacher may not pay attention to what you liked because they're waiting for the 'but', the negatives. In both 2a and 2b the teacher is inclined to be passive while you feed back unless you ask questions.
3(a) 'So I think these are your action points' or 3(b) 'What do you think you need to work on?'	3(a) This gives the teacher no active role in deciding what needs to be worked on. They may act on your suggestions successfully but often they don't. 3(b) This gives the teacher some choice in prioritising what the observer thinks they need to do, but responsibility is minimal.

Malderez and Bodoczky (1999) suggest using a framework for feedback that has different styles and actions in each of the phases. I have adapted their framework (see Table 8.3) to address issues and areas for development first (which lead into setting objectives) and to end by discussing the teacher's strengths. I have found that this helps the observer stay focused on the main points because it stops them going round in circles or going off on unhelpful tangents. This is how the phases work.

Table 8.3 Improved framework for a post-observation discussion

Phase	Commentary
Pre 1. Decide on key points	Have a clear view of the teacher's strengths and write them down. Think about but don't write the features that were less good, prioritising those which have the most negative impact on pupils' progress and well being.
1. Warm-up	Thank the teacher for letting you observe. Give a headline summarising what you thought of the lesson.
2. Teacher's views	Ask the teacher how they thought it went.
3. Areas to develop	Address the weaknesses that the teacher has identified or ones that you consider. Link these to the effects they are having on the pupils.
4. Strengths and successes	Have a relaxed and thorough discussion about the teacher's strengths and the successes of the lesson.

Pre-phase 1: Decide on key points. It's important to go into a post-observation discussion with a clear view of the teacher's strengths, and what you think they need to work on to be even more effective. Make a list of any 'weaknesses' of the lesson. Don't fall into the trap of criticising because you wouldn't have taught it like that – you didn't. Identify weaknesses that impacted on the pupils' progress and well-being. This should stop you raising points that are simply based on your own idiosyncratic feelings. For instance, some people will feel irritated by things such as the teacher pacing up and down, punctuating every sentence with 'er', or speaking in a monotone, but these should not be raised unless they are affecting pupils' learning. You should also consider whether the teacher would be able to change or improve – things like voice and mannerisms are very hard to alter and strike at the very heart of a person.

Phase 1: Warm–up. Thank the teacher for letting you observe. Give a brief headline of what you thought of the lesson – this is what they want to know, so if it went well say so. If it went badly say something reassuring or sympathetic, commenting on the children ('what a lively group') or the subject matter of the lesson for instance ('analogue clock times are so hard to teach'), but not so as to mislead them.

Phase 2: Teacher's views. Ask the teacher how they thought it went, and why. This will give you an insight into how they evaluate their work. If they have exactly the same view of the lesson as you, things are easy. Others will think the lesson successful when you had misgivings, but more often people focus on the things that didn't go well. Either way, this gives you an insight into how they think – and this will determine how you develop the discussion. If they think they're better than you think they are, consider their reasoning – they might be right. If, after listening, you really feel that their needs are even greater than you originally thought, be tougher and clearer in your message. If they're overly self-critical, you need to boost them up, so forget about raising negatives for now. Most teachers say something like 'Well, I was quite pleased with the lesson overall but I wish…'. This naturally leads into a discussion of an area for development.

Phase 3: Area for further development. Having gained more information from the teacher, you need quickly to decide on the most important things to address. Link these to the effects they are having on the pupils.

Probe – why? You will need to probe further, asking questions that guide the teacher's thinking more deeply about the issue. If they come to a straightforward reason that you agree with, you can move to the next phase: thinking about alternatives. Probing questions will occur to you *in situ* but generally they will be 'why' ones such as 'Why do you think that is?' You can then move into the 'how' phase.

Alternatives – how else? When you are in this phase the teacher and you should be discussing alternatives: how to make a specific aspect of their teaching more effective. A key question would be 'How else might you…?' See your role as someone who allows the teacher to reflect and who asks the questions that encourage them to think of the solutions themselves. Ideally the teacher should think up their own solutions, but you can suggest some too. People get very frustrated if you don't.

Objectives – discuss what things should happen, by whom, with what help and by when. Alternatively this could happen later, when there's more time and after some more reflection.

Phase 4: Strengths. Having got the areas for development out of the way you can now have a relaxed discussion about their strengths and the successes of the lesson. Allow a decent amount of time for this – at least five minutes if the total discussion lasts 15 or 20. Actually, I wouldn't discuss so much as tell, because any discussion is likely to revert to negatives again. This is a time for the teacher to sit back and listen, basking in your praise. It's bound to make them feel uncomfortable but persist as it will make the teacher feel boosted and confident. Don't spoil this by mentioning the areas for development again. Use fulsome praise, linking their teaching to the progress and well-being of the children.

This structure takes practice, which it is useful to do in a role-play situation (see Activity 8.2). People with whom I have used the improved framework feel that they were more active, reflective and boosted by the emphasis on their strengths at the end of the discussion. It also seems to take a shorter time than other feedback structures, because there is a tighter focus.

Activity 8.2

Role-play a post-observation discussion

People work in threes, taking turns to be the teacher, the observer and someone watching the discussion. The watcher notes down what things happen in each phase of the discussion. You'll all need to watch a video of some teaching. Try to get hold of the TTA video of Lyndsay that was used earlier for Activity 7.1. The TTA booklets contain the plans, evaluations and work relating to the lessons. This gives the role-play group plenty of information to work with.

To give people experience of the different situations they might find themselves in discussing lessons, in each of the three role-plays the teacher responds differently to the question 'How do you think the lesson went?':

1. The teacher is reflective and open. When asked how she thought the lesson went, she says she dominated too much.

2. The teacher is very hard on herself and thinks she's taught an awful lesson.

3. The teacher thinks she's taught an excellent lesson in which everyone met their learning objective and made progress.

Each role-play should take about 15 minutes and be followed by comments from the watcher and then a brief discussion. The whole activity should take one hour.

Written feedback

Putting pen to paper is something that everyone worries about, and understandably so. When something is written down it becomes permanent and the meanings that readers interpret from it are out of your hands, so you need to be absolutely clear – and that's hard. It's so much easier to raise issues orally because one can use body language, expression and check understanding during an interaction. In writing there are just the words – and they can seem very stark! In this section I shall discuss the pros and cons of different formats and analyse some real written feedback to illustrate some techniques and phrases to use – and ones to avoid.

Most people would agree that written feedback should contain:

- Praise

- Acknowledgement of success

- Identification of strengths

- Identification of an area to develop, that will be useful in future lessons

- Ideas for improvement

There are several sorts of comments in observation feedback:

- Descriptive – relating what happens, but without any evaluation. Some lesson observation notes are purely descriptive, saying things like 'teacher showed me the plan', but with no judgement. This is not helpful.

- Evaluative – judging, e.g. 'very well planned'.

- Advisory – suggestions, e.g. 'Dean and Wayne might behave better if they were separated'.

- Questioning / reflective – there are two sorts of questions: those designed to stimulate thought and get people thinking about an area that could be improved (e.g. 'How could you have avoided the arguments over pencils?'); and genuine questions for clarification – (e.g. 'Why are you ignoring Pasha's behaviour?'). There isn't often a need to ask a genuine question.

Activity 8.3

Textual analysis of an observation

Photocopy Observation 2 and other observation notes in this chapter and underline phrases that are descriptive (D), evaluative (E), questioning (Qr for ones that encourage reflection or Qg for genuine ones) and advisory (A). What can you learn from this?

Activity 8.3 continued

Observation 2: Year 10 DT

<u>Subject and learning objective</u> Technology – graphics – to complete specific pieces of coursework designing, making and researching parfleches; developing problem-solving skills and using lesson time effectively.

Thank you for letting us observe, Bunmi.

Strengths and points

Students settle down to work well, even without explicit instructions from you. They are clearly well trained, which is the result of much hard work over the year.

You move round the students giving individual support where necessary. You give individual instructions, which results in you repeating things. How else could you have used your time to maximum effect?

Your relationships are strong and your manner is respectful and friendly, with lots of positive comments. Your informality is fine but does it encourage high standards?

Resources are well organised so that students know where things are and can use time efficiently.

Assessment for learning – your feedback reassures students. How do you deepen, extend, challenge, encourage the evaluation so crucial in DT?

Students were generally on task though some were working harder than others. Your aim is for the students to finish a piece of coursework – how could you have ensured this or encouraged more of a sense of urgency? Do you know what they achieved? Do they? A plenary would have helped, as would a tight introduction.

End of the lesson – could you raise expectations of tidying?

Voice – friendly throughout but rather than raising your voice at the end of the lesson, would it be good to have a greater formality, use more authority, through speaking more slowly? You ask for silence but don't seem to expect to get it.

Take care what you write

Read Observation 3. This was written as part of a visit on behalf of the local authority to quality-assure induction provision and to judge whether the school's view of their NQTs was accurate. It contains numerous spelling and grammatical errors (that I have drawn attention to in brackets), which is embarrassing as the person who wrote it is an advanced skills teacher. How would you feed back to her on the quality of her work? What do you think of it? Will it help the new teacher develop? Does it give a clear picture of strengths and areas for development? What message does it send the induction tutor in the school about the standard of lesson observation expected?

Observation 3: AST's observation of a NQT in Year 1

Strengths

Objectives were communicated both visually and verbally. You demonstrated through (thorough) knowledge of the subject and materials were appropriate for the lesson e.g. books of the seasons and appropriate vocabulary was displayed and used (grammar). You made the lesson more assessable (accessible) by using 'Harry', the puppet. You drew upon children's previous experiences as the children were able to chant out the days of the weeks and you encouraged children to assist 'Harry' to rearrange the days in the correct order. You used a variety of activities to engage your class. You involved all the children by listening to them and responding appropriately.

You praised your class by asking them to give themselves a clap when they had achieved the correct order of the days. Generally you managed to address poor behaviour and on several occasion(s) you took prompt action however there was a few children who were not noticed for their actions (grammar and clumsy phrasing). All children were on task and knew exactly what they had to do and you had differentiated the work sheet appropriately. Your teaching assistances (assistants) were well informed and had personal plans as an aid to support their individual groups. You made effective use of the time available especially the countdown to end of lesson.

Areas for further development:

- *Although you had work by the computer it was not switched on:*
- *In future you should provide a lesson plan for any lesson observations.*
- *Try to be more consistent: are the children allowed to call out or not?*

Would you agree that the spelling and grammatical errors are so serious that they devalue what the AST is trying to say – and her credibility as an excellent teacher? I'm sure you would, but if we look beyond them to the content of what she's saying, we get a picture of a reasonable lesson, although there is too little detail to be sure of what strengths the teacher has. One presumes that statements like 'Objectives were communicated both visually and verbally' are positive, but more adjectives alongside the description would let us know more. Crucially, we want to know what effect this had on the children: were they clear about exactly what they were learning and why? We don't know.

Looking at the areas for further development, are we clear what the observer means? Does it really matter that the computer wasn't switched on? Maybe it did if children were expected to use it and didn't know how to turn it on, but otherwise it could seem nitpicky. All areas for development should be identified as such because of their impact on pupils' progress. The second point, about providing a copy of the lesson plan for the observer, isn't an area for development so this is not really the place to make such a comment. That could be raised verbally or written as an aside or in parentheses, e.g. 'Thank you for letting me observe – a copy of your plan would have helped (something to remember for next time)'. The last area for development is a significant issue so it needs to come first and be elaborated upon. The use of a question is a good technique here, and likely to go down better than saying 'Don't let people call out'.

Using key questions to structure writing

A *pro forma* with sentence-prompts based on the structure of the lesson (like that in Observation 4) is useful when you have been very specific in helping teachers develop certain aspects, and want to see how they're doing in response to your input. But some prompts may be red herrings, such as 'How good is the start of the lesson?' How do you define 'good' and 'the start', and why is it important? One of the downsides of using this type of format is that it pushes the observer to write only about the things listed. There may be other striking points you'd like to note but for which there's no room. There's also a fair amount of reading that will slow you down. How helpful will it be to the teacher reading it? Very, if they look at this form carefully since they will know precisely what you're looking for; but it could be a little like teaching to the test. If there are positive things to say in response to each of the prompts, will the lesson overall be successful? Will the pupils have learned anything? That's what matters!

Observation 4: Literacy

a. *Is the plan effective, with clear learning objectives and suitable teaching strategies?*	*You provided a detailed plan with differentiated learning objectives and success criteria; these build upon learning from the previous lesson. The level of challenge for the more able pupils was appropriate; they displayed creativity in their responses. Several of the mainstream/supported children I spoke to interpreted the task as a transcription of information from their plan onto a different template. Have they explored the features of this genre? Were there any opportunities where you could have used partner work/dialogue in the lesson?*
b. *How good is the teacher's command of areas of learning and subjects?*	*You selected and used some good resources for this lesson. Well done for clarifying the misapprehension from yesterday's lesson. Marking in children's books is generally used to good effect and there were some examples of individual targets and areas for development.*
c. *How well does the learning environment support good learning and teaching?*	*The learning environment is outstanding! Attractive displays celebrate children's work and are refreshed regularly. Resources are organised efficiently and the children readily accessed resources such as dictionaries and rulers.*
d. *How good is the start of the lesson?*	*The children settled quickly and the learning objectives and success criteria were shared. There was a clear purpose based on previous learning.*
e. *How well does the teacher interest, encourage, engage and challenge pupils?*	*The activities were interesting and the children were keen to discuss what they were doing. They generally worked independently and sought support where needed.*

f. How effectively is behaviour managed?	Behaviour was excellent. The children worked quietly and demonstrated considerable maturity.
g. How effectively does the teacher promote equality of opportunity and inclusion?	The contributions of all pupils were valued and encouraged, e.g. M was very happy to share the outcomes from his task. The more able pupils were set an appropriate level of challenge and it was pleasing to note that you deployed your teaching assistant to support these.
h. Is effective use made of additional adults?	Teaching assistant had a very clear view of what was to be achieved; she had received copies of planning and was aware of your expectations. She supported her group well and they produced some imaginative work with her guidance.
i. How effectively does the teacher use the plenary to reinforce learning and assess understanding?	The plenary was used to revisit the learning objectives and success criteria. A number of children read out their work and seemed pleased with their accomplishments. Consider using the plenary as an opportunity for interaction and peer assessment.
j. How effectively does the teacher assess pupils' work thoroughly and constructively?	Pupils are set targets and there are prompts within the learning environment to support self-assessment.

Writing about lessons that are less than satisfactory

> We have a teacher with big control problems but instead of looking at what she's doing, she blames the children and the parents. No amount of support makes much of a difference to her. (Induction tutor)

Writing about lessons that are less than satisfactory is hard. When you're trying to develop a teacher who is not very effective, there needs to be a balance between praise for what is going well, and clarity about what needs improvement. The trouble is that with a less effective teacher it's hard to find positive things to say and it can be hard to diagnose which of the many problems will be the key one to address.

Most teachers' egos are very fragile, by and large, no matter how experienced they are, or how big and strong they seem. Most of us are highly critical of our performance and don't need anyone to labour over weaknesses. A hint, an idea of what could have been better, an apposite question will be enough to make most teachers scurry away, shed some tears and improve. So take care over how you phrase criticisms: be precise but subtle and use hard evidence, as can be seen in these comments around the use of time in a special school maths lesson:

> *You planned for the introduction to last for five minutes, and it actually took four minutes for Dale to give out all the bottles. Whilst it is good for him to be engaged in such helpful behaviours, the time taken to hand out resources resulted in many of the pupils losing a degree of attention.*

This style is a good way to get a difficult message across, and to give the teacher food for thought. The level of detail suggests that the observer knows the pupils and what is best for them. It would be hard to argue with the points raised because they are so linked to the effect of teaching on learning.

Sometimes, though, a tougher approach is used – and it can work or it can be counter-productive. What do you think of this induction tutor's actions and feedback?

> *When you began the lesson (over 5 minutes in), your opening words were, 'The title's on the board for those of you who can be bothered.' That was it. I stepped in, not really wanting to undermine you, and asked pupils to stop writing (those who were, at least). I addressed the whole group and said that I had never known a teacher begin a lesson in such a negative way. I said that it gave me some insight into things that had gone before this lesson and I was not impressed that you had resorted to speaking to the class in this way. It was clear that your expectations of the group as a whole were extremely low and this type of statement is an invitation to pupils not to do any work. You must try to be more positive with the whole class and enthuse them. They are there to learn: it is not up to them whether they choose to participate. I asked them to put the title and date into their books and waited for you to continue.*

Most teachers will benefit from a subtle approach of support with a gentle hint of pressure to make things improve. Others agree when weaknesses are pointed out but seem incapable to remedy them, such as this induction tutor who said:

> *I am not sure that Sue is actually reflecting carefully or deeply enough to affect change in her practice. She is ready to admit her mistakes but tends to repeat them.*

Occasionally, however, one comes across teachers who think they're fine (great, even) when they're not and are oblivious to hints and any subtleness. With such a person you need a different approach: one that gives a very clear picture of the position, which is not sandwiched or hidden within positive points. What do you think of how this has been written? It was written after discussing the last observation of a failing NQT's induction year:

> *We had a very long discussion about the lesson and your teaching in general. As a result, it is my opinion that you are not demonstrating that you meet the standards for the satisfactory completion of the induction period. In addition to the concerns from the lesson listed above, our discussion has made me worried about your lack of understanding of pupils' levels; reflection and insight into the effectiveness of your teaching; and responsibility for your professional development; and the fact that you have not acted upon advice and or carried out the very specific action points.*
> (Induction consultant, Term 3)

Most induction tutors find it hard to be tough, but you need to think of the pupils. They deserve the best and we need to help teachers develop so that they get it.

HAPTER 9

Assessment

- Reviewing progress at half-terms

- Being assessed at the end of term

- Assessment meeting

- Evidence

- Monitoring and support

- The recommendation

- Writing against the standards

- The new teacher's comment

- The final assessment report

Induction exists to help new teachers – even the assessment side of it. I say this because I've known some schools that assess in a punitive way, not in one which helps a new teacher develop by giving a clear picture of their progress towards the standards.

School leaders and induction tutors often find a tension between the Ofsted inspection criteria and using the core standards to judge a new teacher. There is a difference! Inspectors focus on the progress pupils make, but this is not explicitly mentioned in any core standards. Standard C30 comes closest: 'Teach engaging and motivating lessons informed by well-grounded expectations of learners and designed to raise levels of attainment'. But note that the NQT is only required to *plan*, not deliver, improved levels of attainment. The core standards are about teaching: but there are no standards that say that children must make progress as a result of teaching. Having said that, if a teacher were meeting all the standards to a good degree I'm sure pupils would be making progress. So, if pupil progress is disappointing, look more closely at the standards and exactly how the teacher is meeting them – perhaps expectations are not quite high enough.

Reviewing progress at half-terms

New teachers should review their progress at half-terms with their induction tutor, as well as being assessed at the end of each term. There's no official form for this, but I suggest using Template 5 in the Appendix. This is a time to take stock and appreciate what you've learned and how far you've come on your journey to being the best teacher in the world. What's going well in your progress towards the standards? What needs to be better? Maybe you've had to go off course from the way you want to teach for all manner of pragmatic reasons – say, the kids behave better in rows but that's not how you want to work in the long term. Most of you will be making satisfactory or better progress. You'll always be thinking about what's going to help you be a better class teacher, but don't get distracted from this most complex and important journey. Running clubs and taking other roles in the school can be an unnecessary and lengthy diversion.

Look at your induction entitlement. Did you get it all? Did you use it well? If not, you need to address why and the issues to improve the situation. Be clear about what support you want. Make sure that your programme, like Julian's in Chapter 2 (see Table 2.8), is individualised, is focused on what you need to get better at and has the right balance of support, monitoring and assessment. His objectives are clear, and broken down into bite-sized activities and specific support, because he's thought about what he needs to improve and what help he'll need. He's arranged help from not only the induction tutor but also the assessment coordinator.

Being assessed at the end of term

For many people the assessment process is straightforward and reassuring. Standardised forms have to be filled in and sent to the appropriate body within ten days of the meeting, although ABs will usually set their own deadlines for reports.

Unfortunately there are cases of poor practice:

> The induction tutor, whom I never had any sessions with, eventually completed the paperwork for the two terms on my last day at the school. I didn't know that I was able to make any comments on the forms. I was just handed the papers and told to sign them! It was not even original paperwork – they had none in stock and so requested faxed copies from another school and it was printed off on the old style shiny fax roll, complete with another school's details across the top! (NQT, Term 3)

One wonders what happened to the 14 per cent of NQTs in the national evaluation of induction who didn't have an assessment report at the end of each term (Totterdell *et al.*, 2002). How did the AB know how they were doing? Did the NQTs pass their induction period satisfactorily, or did the outstanding paperwork mean that they did not? One NQT's first term assessment meeting and report did not take place until the end of the second term. Another said 'I have never seen the written reports'. One headteacher told a NQT at the end-of-year final assessment meeting that she had failed induction. She had no inkling that this was a possibility and had passed the first two terms' assessments. Again, it shouldn't happen: according to the regulations, the half-termly reviews of progress and termly assessments should give a clear picture so that there are no surprises.

Assessment meeting

> *I'm currently off work with the flu and have not yet had an assessment meeting with my tutor – although I have been told that I have passed the first term. What happens about the forms that need to be filled in and sent off to the local authority: is there a deadline? Will my first term count?*
> (NQT, Term 2)

The three formal assessment meetings are very important and valuable in reviewing progress. They should be held towards the end of each term, and are the forum for the termly assessment reports to be discussed and written. Schools are obviously busy at the end of term, so put a date in the diary for your assessment meetings with the head and induction tutor. Choose a date that is convenient to all and make sure that at least a week's notice is given. Think carefully about a realistic start and finish time – it will be important to feel fresh. The length of the meeting will depend on the degree of agreement about your performance and how much preparatory work on the report has been done. A straightforward case for which all are well briefed should take not much more than half an hour. Holding the meeting in your classroom may give you a feeling of control that you may not have in the headteacher's office. It also means that there is easy access to further evidence, such as pupils' work.

If you or the induction tutor is ill and the meeting doesn't happen or the report doesn't get written, it's not the end of the world. The term will still count towards your induction period. Someone should contact the AB and let them know that the report will be delayed and you'll need to make sure your assessment report and meeting are at the top of the agenda at the start of the new term, so that progress is not delayed.

During the assessment meeting suggest additions or revisions to the wording on the form so that you feel it's accurate. You should be clear about your strengths and areas for further development as well as what your targets are and what support is planned.

Evidence

Many people worry about what evidence they must show to pass induction. Some schools expect NQTs to keep teaching practice-level folders of evidence (Bubb *et al.*, 2002), but this is unnecessary. You keep enough paperwork as a class teacher. If you've been teaching for a term you will have lots of evidence for the standards: you will have been setting targets, planning, teaching, assessing, managing pupils, using individual education plans, working with support staff, talking to parents, implementing school policies and taking an active part in your professional development. You don't need to collect any extra evidence – mind you, look through the standards to check that there aren't any gaps. Don't worry about standards that don't apply to you – if you don't teach pupils with special needs, you can't contribute to individual education plans.

Monitoring and support

The headteacher is responsible for ticking the kinds of monitoring and support that have been in place during the term: the ten per cent reduced timetable; your career entry and development profile; a plan of support; discussions with your induction tutor to set targets and review progress; observations of your teaching every half term; observations by you of other teachers; and an assessment meeting. If they haven't all happened, they shouldn't be ticked. It's the only way that your AB will know you're not getting your entitlement.

New teachers sometimes ask 'Is there anything I can do to let the AB know my situation without dropping my school in it?' Professionally worded comments on the assessment form and phone calls to the person in charge of NQTs at the AB should be made. What you mustn't do is allow your development to suffer – or to risk failing. You are a professional and are expected to speak up for yourself in resolving issues.

The recommendation

You can't 'fail' your first or second term on induction because it's only the judgement at the end of the third term that really matters. The form for the first and second terms requires the head-teacher to tick one of two statements: either

> The above named teacher's progress indicates that he/she will be able to meet the requirements for the satisfactory completion of the induction period

or

> The above named teacher's current progress suggests that he/she may not be able to meet the requirements for the satisfactory completion of the induction period.

You should know if you're at risk of failure because observations of your teaching and the first and/or second term's reports would have said your progress was unsatisfactory. If they did not, you are unlikely to be anywhere near failing. The system does not allow for last-minute shocks. To be sure, check with your head.

It isn't the end of the world not to be making satisfactory progress in the first term, but it is a clear warning and should ensure targeted support. If your progress is dodgy, the school and AB need to ensure that support and monitoring mechanisms are in place to give you every possible chance of success. If you aren't making satisfactory progress after the first or second term, the assessment report and meeting should mean that you're clear about what you have to do to improve.

If you're not making satisfactory progress by the end of the second term you have every reason to panic because it doesn't bode well. In theory, you should be able to pull things together in the remaining third term and your school should move heaven and earth to help you do so. In practice, problems are very hard to turn around. If you're in this position, get advice, especially from your union. You might want to leave the school and complete your third term at another time and place. With lessons learned, a fresh start may be just what you need.

Writing against the standards

The induction tutor will probably be responsible for writing the reports. Make sure you are happy with what is written about you – that it is a fair reflection of you – by self-assessing using Template 5 in the Appendix.

Activity 9.1

Analysing a report – professional attributes

Using Table 9.1, analyse the Professional Attitudes section of Lu's first term's report.

1. Which standards does this report cover?

2. What do you like about the way this report is written?

3. What could be better?

4. What are the learning points for you?

Lu shows a professional attitude and has developed excellent working relationships with the Key Stage 1 staff. She is a popular member of the team and works well with her parallel teacher and teaching assistant giving valuable input during planning sessions. She has high expectations for all of the children and is committed to raising standards. Lu has been observed by a number of internal and external members of staff and has used feedback from observations to develop her practice. Lu has attended regular staff development meetings, inset days and NQT meetings where she is developing a range of skills and knowledge including target setting, levelling and subject knowledge. She has shown an interest in using her skills to contribute to extra curricular activities for the children. Lu uses her professional judgement to assess situations and will call on relevent professional support and advice where necessary. Lu held her first parents'/carers' evening where she shared the children's successes, set targets and gave advice and ideas of how parents/carers could support their child at home. She follows school procedures and policies with regard to behaviour and health and safety. Lu sets a good example to children and adults she is always well organised and conducts herself in a professional manner at all times.

Activity 9.1 continued

Table 9.1 Analysing an assessment report in relationship to the standards

Standards – professional attributes (TDA, 2007b)	What does report say?
C1 Have high expectations of children and young people including a commitment to ensuring that they can achieve their full educational potential and to establishing fair, respectful, trusting, supportive and constructive relationships with them.	
C2 Hold positive values and attitudes and adopt high standards of behaviour in their professional role.	
C3 Maintain an up-to-date knowledge and understanding of the professional duties of teachers and the statutory framework within which they work, and contribute to the development, implementation and evaluation of the policies and practice of their workplace, including those designed to promote equality of opportunity.	
C4 (a) Communicate effectively with children, young people and colleagues. (b) Communicate effectively with parents and carers, conveying timely and relevant information about attainment, objectives, progress and well-being. (c) Recognise that communication is a two-way process and encourage parents and carers to participate in discussions about the progress, development and well-being of children and young people.	
C5 Recognise and respect the contributions that colleagues, parents and carers can make to the development and well-being of children and young people, and to raising their levels of attainment.	
C6 Have a commitment to collaboration and co-operative working where appropriate.	
C7 Evaluate their performance and be committed to improving their practice through appropriate professional development.	
C8 Have a creative and constructively critical approach towards innovation; being prepared to adapt their practice where benefits and improvements are identified.	
C9 Act upon advice and feedback and be open to coaching and mentoring.	

Activity 9.2

Analysing a report – professional skills

Analyse the professional skills section of Rosemary's second term report

1. What do you like about the way this report is written?

2. What questions might the appropriate body want to ask the induction tutor?

3. What could be better?

4. What are the learning points for you?

Professional Skills

Rosemary is making good progress in this area. She has secure subject knowledge and can use key objectives to plan, resource and assess every lesson to a high standard. The lessons she prepares are exciting and varied – the children therefore are immediately

Activity 9.2

engaged with the learning. During an RE lesson which I observed which included film, images and music, the children clapped when they were shown what their activity would be! More important, at the beginning when she linked the learning, following talk-partners, she asked the children what they had been learning about, the majority of the class had their hand up with something to say. The vocabulary they used to describe their learning was excellent. She takes great care to link the learning and relate the objectives to real life. She has a good relationship with all the children in the class and is aware of needs in relation to gender and ethnicity. Rosemary has taken part in peer observations as well as observing good practice across the school and externally. Following these observations Rosemary quickly transfers good practice seen to enhance the learning within her own classroom. Behaviour management within her classroom has improved greatly during the first two terms; however, this is still an area for Rosemary to work on. After a term of getting to know the children better and being able now to recognise potential 'trouble times' during the day Rosemary has carefully thought about how to intercept these. During the coming term she will continue to anticipate and manage behaviour – particularly developing strategies to allow smooth transition from one activity to another, or from the carpet to the tables. Through observations Rosemary has collected a range of behaviour management strategies which she intends to use. This will be further supported next term through continued peer observation partnerships, demonstration lessons from an AST and whole staff INSET.

The new teacher's comment

NQTs can choose whether or not to make a comment on the report, and have a box in which to write. I think you should write something since the whole emphasis in induction is on NQTs being proactive and reflective. Some NQTs say which parts of their induction programme have been most useful; others defend themselves; others write about what they feel are their strengths and areas for development. Perhaps something like this would be appropriate:

> I agree with my report. My progress has been hampered by the lack of support that my induction tutor has been able to give me because of her other duties. I have only had a reduced timetable in the weeks of –– I hope that next term I will get release time regularly in order to observe and learn from other colleagues and make progress in developing my teaching. (NQT, Term 1)

Sign the form, check it's posted and received by the AB and keep a copy for your professional portfolio.

The final assessment report

The last report doesn't require any writing, if you have met the core standards, but you should discuss how well you're meeting the standards. Use the time to get a clear picture of your strengths and successes, and celebrate them. Discuss what you should develop in your second year when you get slotted into the school's performance management arrangements.

In cases of either a successful or a failing NQT, the headteacher is only making a recommendation to the AB. It is up to them to make the final decision. In the case of failures, many ABs will want to observe the NQT, but this is not statutory. The AB is responsible for making sure that the assessment of the NQT was accurate and reliable, that the NQT's objectives were set appropriately and that they were supported. The AB can grant extensions to the induction period but only in exceptional circumstances, where:

> for reasons unforeseen and/or beyond the control of one or more of the parties involved, it is unreasonable to expect the NQT to meet the requirements by the end of their induction support programme, or there is insufficient evidence on which a decision can be made about whether the Induction Standards have been met. (DfES, 2003a: para. 126)

NQTs can appeal to the General Teaching Council against the decision to extend the induction period or to fail them.

The assessment process should leave you happy to know your strengths and be clear about your areas for development. This sets you up well for the rest of your career – your continuing professional development and performance management.

CHAPTER 10

What next?

- Transition Point 3

- Pay

- Contracts

- Performance management

When you're nearing the end of your induction year, take stock of how far you've come and where you want to move on to. This chapter has a few ideas about using the Transition Point 3 discussion to help, before explaining about how teachers' pay and contracts work, and it ends by looking at how to make performance management work for your career and professional development.

Transition Point 3

Remember your career entry and development profile? Look back to Transition Point 2 and see how far you've come: I bet you hardly recognise yourself! In the Transition Point 3 discussion with your induction tutor, you'll review this year and think about the next. Use the following list of questions to structure your preparations for this discussion:

1. Thinking back over your induction period, what do you feel have been your most significant achievements as a NQT?

   - What have been your key learning moments?

   - What prompted your learning on these occasions?

   - Which aspects of your induction support programme have you particularly valued and why?

2. How have you built on the strengths you identified at the end of your initial teacher training?

   - What evidence is there of your progress in these areas?

3. When you look back over your induction action plans and your records of review meetings, which objectives do you feel have been achieved and why?

   ■ Are there any areas where you are less satisfied with your progress?

   ■ Why is this?

   ■ What further actions will you take in these areas?

   ■ What further preparation or support do you feel you will need?

4. Have any of the objectives, aspirations and goals that you outlined at transition points 1 and 2 not been addressed during your induction period?

   ■ How could you take these forward into the next stage of your career?

5. Thinking ahead to the class(es) you will teach and the responsibilities you will be taking on next year, what do you feel are the priorities for your professional development over the next two or three years?

6. What options are you currently considering for professional and career progression?

   ■ Why are you interested in extending your expertise in this way?

   ■ What could you do to help you move towards achieving these ambitions?
   (TDA, 2007a)

Do give feedback on how the school's induction provision has worked for you. There are many saints who do a splendid job for NQTs, so boost them with heartfelt and public praise, because other people have had dire experiences. That needs recording too, so that future teachers get a better deal.

Pay

Did you go into teaching because of the money? Probably not, but salary is an important issue, especially when so many new teachers feel burdened by having to repay their student loans. According to a survey by the Association of Teachers and Lecturers (ATL), over a quarter of NQTs feel heavily burdened by debt and, worryingly, over a fifth of them are considering leaving teaching because of it. These statistics are not surprising considering that 40 per cent of those surveyed qualified with debts in excess of £10,000 (see Table 10.1).

Table 10.1 New teachers' debt when qualified as a teacher (ATL, 2007)

None	20.7%
£1–£5,000	19.9%
£5,000–£10,000	19%
£10,000–£15,000	22.5%
£15,000–£20,000	13.7%
£20,000+	4.2%

Teachers' pay is really confusing because there have been so many changes. The figures in this book relate to 2007, but if you want to keep up to date go to your employer or union website.

For a start, there are different pay scales for

- unqualified teachers

- main scale

- upper scale

- advanced skills teachers

- leadership group

- headteachers.

Within each of these there are four separate scales depending on whether you work in inner, outer or the fringe of London, or elsewhere in England and Wales. There's nearly £4,000 difference between the areas, so it pays to be strategic. Of the capital's 33 boroughs, those that border a county are classed as outer London, and all others are inner. Ealing, Haringey and Merton are classed as inner London, even though they're not in the inner ring. There are no easy rules about fringe payments but you get it as far out as places like Welwyn and Hatfield.

If you're not yet qualified, because for instance you're still training or you've yet to pass your skills tests to get QTS, you'll be paid on the unqualified ten-point scale. At the moment this ranges from £14,391 to £22,761 (£18,099 to £26,466 in inner London).

All newly qualified teachers start on the six-point main scale (Table 10.2). Confusingly, some people refer to its previous names: the common pay spine (CPS) or teachers' pay scale (TPS). Most people start on M1 and after six years will be at the top of the scale and so entitled to cross the threshold and move to the upper pay scale. You move up a point every September, subject to satisfactory progress. Late starters, part-timers and temporary teachers go up a point if they've been employed for at least 26 weeks during the year.

Table 10.2 Main scale teacher pay, 1 September 2007

	England and Wales	Inner London	Outer London	Fringe
M1	£20,133	£24,168	£23,118	£21,102
M2	£21,726	£25,548	£24,501	£22,692
M3	£23,472	£27,327	£26,247	£24,438
M4	£25,278	£29,328	£28,053	£26,250
M5	£27,270	£31,584	£30,432	£28,239
M6	£29,427	£33,936	£32,751	£30,393

Source: www.teachernet.gov.uk/management/payandperformance/pay/.

You can start higher up the scale than M1 in recognition of 'relevant' experience, though relevance is interpreted differently by different schools. An ATL survey (January 2007) of 361 NQTs in England and Wales found that 43.5 per cent were paid above M1: 27.7 per cent at M2, 7.2 per cent at M3, 4.4 per cent at M4, 1.9 per cent at M5, and 2.2 per cent at M6.

Once awarded, your position on the main scale can't be reduced even if you move schools, so it's important to negotiate the best starting point that you can as soon as you're offered a job. But you've got to be proactive about stating your case based on your previous experience of working with children or in a role deemed to be appropriate to teaching. There are no hard-and-fast rules to what you'll get as it's down to the discretion of school governing bodies. Basically, it's a lottery: the same person could get paid on M3 in one school but only M1 in another, which is a difference of £3,000. I know a new business studies teacher who's on M5 but a 46-year-old mother of four with 20 years of experience as a nursery nurse and a first-class BEd who's on only M1 because she didn't ask for more. I hope the former is worth the extra £7,000 a year, but it just doesn't seem fair to me. When you reach M6 you can cross the threshold and move onto the upper pay scale, or if you have evidence that you are an outstanding teacher you might want to apply for advanced skills teacher status, which has its own scale the top of which is nearly equivalent to a leadership post.

Deductions

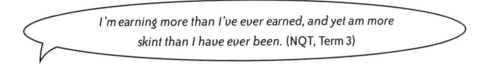

I'm earning more than I've ever earned, and yet am more skint than I have ever been. (NQT, Term 3)

Before you start planning how to spend your hard-earned cash, remember that you get only about two-thirds of your salary as take-home pay because there are deductions for:

- tax (have to pay);
- National Insurance (have to pay);
- pension, also called superannuation (strongly advised to pay);
- General Teaching Council membership (have to pay in state schools);
- union subscription (optional but highly advisable);
- student loan repayments (have to pay if you took out a loan).

Tax is paid at 20 per cent (from April 2008) on any money earned over the personal allowance of £5,225. Any income over £34,600 gets taxed at 40 per cent. All but the lowest-paid work incurs 11 per cent National Insurance deductions. You'll pay 6.4 per cent to fund your teachers' pension, and many people make additional voluntary contributions to boost it. The employer contributes 14.1 per cent to it, so it's much better than a personal pension. Despite this, the ATL have found that 11 per cent of the new teachers they surveyed had not opted into the scheme, generally because they felt that they could not afford to invest in a pension.

All teachers in the maintained sector must register with the GTC of the country they work in. In England this costs £33 a year, but you don't lose out as local authorities pay an extra £33 to teachers through their salary. The £33 via the local authority is subject to tax and National Insurance, but you can claim tax relief on professional subscriptions so the GTC fee is virtually free. In Scotland, you pay £50 for your application to be assessed by the GTCS then £55 for the first year and £40 for each subsequent year.

Tax relief can be claimed on union membership. You don't have to join a union, but it's strongly advised. Full union fees are in the region of £140 a year, but each of the unions offers free membership for student teachers, as well as discounted rates and special introductory offers for new members. For instance, the ATL gives free membership for the first year, the NASUWT gives half-price membership for two years, and the NUT gives one term free followed by half-price membership for two years. Most people join all the unions as a student when they're free, and then choose the one that suits them best. If you can't decide between them, there are benefits to joining the union that has most members in your first school. There's safety in numbers!

Repayments on student loans kick in when people have earned over £15,000 in a tax year, which is from 6 April to 5 April. Go to www.slc.co.uk for more information.

Contracts

Many union issues are to do with contracts. Teachers in maintained schools are employed under the terms of the *School Teachers' Pay and Conditions Document* (STPCD) which is published by HMSO and updated annually at www.teachernet.gov.uk/management/payandperformance/pay/. This contains information on salary scales, but the *Conditions of Service for School Teachers in England & Wales*, which is known colloquially as the 'Burgundy Book' and is accessible via the same URL, is very useful too. This contains information about sick pay, maternity leave and such like. All the unions produce handy summaries with a wealth of the most useful information and often give them out at new teacher induction or welcome sessions. A careful read may stop you making erroneous complaints. For instance, some new teachers think that they're exempt from covering for absent colleagues. Unfortunately not: your duties include 'supervising and so far as practicable teaching any pupils whose teacher is not available to teach them'. However, there is a limit of 38 hours per year and paragraph 76.4 states that 'a teacher shall not be required to carry out any other duties, including the provision of cover, during PPA time'.

By the way, a spoken offer and acceptance of a teaching post establish a legal contract even if there is nothing in writing to confirm the agreement. You shouldn't renege on the contract. Theoretically schools could sue if you do but, in practice, it's probably too much trouble and expense for them to do so. Nevertheless, you'll get a bad name: the education grapevine works very efficiently, so in the future you may reap the consequences of less than perfect behaviour. Until you're sure of the exact terms of the post accept 'subject to contract' so that you can negotiate the best deal. Remember, though, to be very professional about this so that you don't look greedy or cheeky.

Many schools try to fob new teachers off with a temporary or fixed-term contract rather than a permanent one. Temporary contracts result in insecurity, inequality and low status. You'll find it hard to get loans or a mortgage. So apply for permanent posts, unless you have very little option. Regardless of whether you work on a full-time, part-time, temporary or permanent basis, once you've completed 12 months of continuous service with the same employer, you have the right not to be unfairly dismissed. When you're on induction you shouldn't be asked to take on management responsibilities, but I've known NQTs appointed as heads of department or SENCOs, all of which are completely unreasonable demands on someone fresh from training.

The pay and conditions arrangements for new appointees to academies or independent schools are not necessarily identical to those under the STPCD and the Burgundy Book. Even though they're state-funded, each academy is able to decide for itself the form of pay and conditions for newly appointed teachers, so you'll need to read your contract closely. Look especially at teachers' working time, such as requirements to do lunch duty, cover, and clubs and find out if you get the ten per cent PPA time.

Performance management

Thinking ahead to what you're going to teach and the responsibilities you'll be taking on next year, what early professional development will you need? Research done on behalf of the TDA (Thewlis, 2006) revealed that 86 per cent of second-year teachers take on additional responsibilities, but six out of ten receive little or no support to prepare them for new responsibilities. Two-fifths of teachers found that their Transition Point 3 training objectives were not incorporated into plans for their second year.

Performance management is the statutory procedure for making sure that all teachers after completing induction discuss their teaching, professional development, career plans and how to be more effective. Done well, it should make you feel valued, give you a clear picture about your work and help you develop, but it takes time, skills and commitment, on the part of both the reviewer and you.

Someone who knows your work will be nominated to be your 'reviewer'. You will have one formal meeting each year, which has two parts: reviewing the past year and then planning the next. In reviewing the past year, ask yourself what's gone well. Look at the main elements of your job description, your previous objectives and professional development to consider not only what you've done but also the impact of your work. Use evidence from as broad a base as possible, such as:

- feedback from pupils, parents and colleagues,

- analysis of test results,

- self-evaluation,

- observations of your teaching,

- planning, evaluations,

- work samples showing progress and the impact of assessment for learning.

Use benchmarking data to compare the impact of your work with others in a similar context nationally and locally. For instance, if you're in London, use the Family of Schools to compare your work with other schools in your 'family'.

In planning the next year, the following are useful questions to think about:

- What would you like to improve?

- Why? What's the current picture?

- How does this fit in with the school improvement plan?

- How does this fit in with your career plan and any standards you're working towards?

- How will you know that things have improved, in about a year?

- What do you need to do to meet this objective?

- What support from the school, including professional development, will help you?

- How should your progress and its impact be monitored?

An outcome of this meeting is the draft performance review statement, which should be given to you for your agreement within five days. The completed review statement is passed to the headteacher within ten days. During the year, you and your reviewer should keep an eye on your professional development and progress towards the objectives. Now that there is a limit of three hours' worth of lesson observation in any year, it's important to get the most out of it. At the end of the year you should do a formal review of your progress together and then set some more objectives for the next year.

You'll discuss your progress at the end of the performance management cycle. The following structure, which is illustrated in the example below, may help:

What I have done. Prepare well for this by having records of what you did. Don't forget to include any unplanned actions – new ideas and strategies are being invented all the time. If things haven't gone to plan, or had the intended impact, analyse why. Whatever the reason, learn from the experience for the future so that you develop into the best teacher you can be.

How I know I've made progress towards the objective. Reflect not just on whether you have met the objective but on how far you are meeting it. Most importantly, have evidence of what has improved, and what the impact is. Analysing why some things worked better than others is important in helping you make the best professional development choices in the future: we are all different and learn in different ways. Sometimes it's not easy to know exactly what helped because of the complexity of learning and teaching. Also, development is gradual and not always straightforward. That's where your reviewer's knowledge of your work and overview of your progress will help.

What if my objectives haven't been met? Don't panic: you're bound to have made some progress and that will be useful to discuss alongside reasons why an objective hasn't been fully met. Perhaps it was too ambitious or circumstances changed. Your school's CPD coordinator should have been given a copy of the professional support planned, and you need to be proactive throughout the year in making sure that what was planned actually happens. You shouldn't be held responsible if the professional support didn't happen.

Next steps. If your objective is fully met, there may be nothing more to do in this area. However, most development needs a bit of attention in order to sustain it and it may be that although you've made progress you now want to make more. Discuss your priorities with your reviewer.

Here's an example of a review of one objective:

Objective: To manage stress more effectively

What I have done:

- *as a result of the coaching received, I am better at setting myself more realistic targets and rewarding myself when I meet them;*

- *my own health and well-being have been improved by walking a kilometre a day, going to an exercise class once a week and drinking water at school instead of coffee;*

- *I make lists of what needs to be done, with time allocations;*

- *I spend fewer hours at school, but use them more efficiently;*

- *I use my diary to timetable when tasks need to be done by and I use PPA time more productively;*

- *I deal more calmly with behaviour issues in the classroom, and spend less time on them.*

How I know I manage stress more effectively:

- *I'm less tired and my blood pressure has gone down (from 150/95 to 135/80);*

- *pupils and colleagues say that I appear happier.*

Next steps:

- *although I try to distance myself, pupils' out-of-school problems still upset and worry me;*

- *I think I'm in a good position to support others manage stress. (Bubb, 2007: 9)*

Conclusion

Used intelligently and creatively, induction and performance management should be an ongoing professional conversation: the chance to reflect, celebrate achievements, solve problems and move forward. Make it work for you by investing in yourself: thousands of children and young people will benefit.

APPENDIX

Templates

Template 1: An action plan to meet an objective

Name: Date: Date objective to be met:

Objective:

Success criteria	Actions	When	Progress

Review:

Template 2: Classroom observation – in-class jottings

Teacher:		Obs focus:
Observer:		Class:
Support staff:		Subject:
Date: Start end		Learning obj:

Prompts	ok	Comments and evidence. What impact does teaching have on pupils?
Relationships		
Expectations		
School policies		
Communication		
Collaboration		
Subject knowledge		
Planning		
Objectives		
T&L strategies		
Behaviour		
Organisation		
Resources		
Use of time		
Questioning		
Motivating		
Differentiation		
Other adults		
Assessment		
Plenary		
Learning environment		*Time: Pupils on task:* *Time: Pupils on task:*

Template 3: Classroom observation – summary

Teacher:	Obs focus:
Observer:	Class:
Support staff:	Subject:
Date: Start: end:	Learning obj:

Strengths of the lesson

Areas for further development

Teacher's comment

Signatures:

Template 4: Professional review meeting – half-termly

Date & time of meeting:

Agenda:

- Progress in teaching overall and on current objectives – things that are going well and what to improve

- How is Induction going?

Progress in teaching overall and on current objectives – things that are going well

Progress in teaching overall and on current objectives – things to improve

How is Induction going? (meetings, cover for and use of reduced timetable, objectives)

Date of next review meeting

Signatures

Template 5: Evaluating progress against the standards to inform the end-of-term assessment

Standards	Going well	Needs improvement
Professional attributes		
Professional knowledge and understanding		
Professional skills		

Photocopiable *Successful Induction for New Teachers*, Paul Chapman Publishing © Sara Bubb, 2007

REFERENCES

Association of Teachers and Lecturers (2007) *New Teacher Debt Survey*. London: ATL.

Bleach, K. (1999) *The Induction and Mentoring of Newly Qualified Teachers*. London: David Fulton.

Bleach, K., Adeghe, A., Rhodes, C. and Roxborough, H. (2004) *Managing the Reflective Induction of Newly Qualified Teachers*. Wolverhampton: University of Wolverhampton School of Education.

Bleach, K. (2006) Sneyd School induction materials. Wolverhampton: Sneyd School.

Bubb, S. (2000) *The Effective Induction of Newly Qualified Primary Teachers: An Induction Tutor's Handbook*. London: David Fulton.

Bubb, S. (2003) *The Insider's Guide to Early Professional Development: Succeed in Your First Five Years*. London: RoutledgeFalmer.

Bubb, S. (2005a) *Helping Teachers Develop*. London: Sage/Paul Chapman.

Bubb, S. (2005b) 'Tum's the word'. *Times Educational Supplement*, 9 September.

Bubb, S. (2007) *Making Performance Management Work for You*. London: ATL.

Bubb, S. and Earley, P. (2004) *Managing Teacher Workload: Work-Life Balance and Wellbeing*. London: Sage/Paul Chapman.

Bubb, S. and Earley, P. (2007) *Leading and Managing Continuing Professional Development: Developing People, Developing Schools*, 2nd edn. London: Sage/Paul Chapman.

Bubb, S. and Hoare, P. (2001) *Performance Management – Monitoring Teaching in the Primary School*. London: David Fulton.

Bubb, S., Heilbronn, R., Jones, C., Totterdell, M. and Bailey, M. (2002) *Improving Induction*. London: RoutledgeFalmer.

Cordingley, P., Bell, M., Thomason, S. and Firth, A. (2005) *The Impact of Collaborative Continuing Professional Development (CPD) on Classroom Teaching and Learning*. London: EPPI-Centre, Institute of Education.

Dennison, B. and Kirk, R. (1990) *Do, Review, Learn, Apply: A Simple Guide to Experiential Learning*. Oxford: Blackwell.

Department for Education and Skills (2003a) *The Induction Support Programme for Newly Qualified Teachers*. London: DfES.

Department for Education and Skills (2003b) *Every Child Matters: Next Steps*. London: DfES.

Department for Education and Skills (2005) *Common Core of Skills and Knowledge for the Children's Workforce*. Nottingham: DfES Publications. http://www.everychildmatters.gov.uk/deliveringservices/commoncore/ (accessed May 2007).

Department for Education and Skills (2007) *Chartered London Teacher Guidance*. London: DfES.

General Teaching Council for England (2006a) *Peer Observation*. Birmingham: GTC. http://www.gtce.org.uk/shared/contentlibs/126802/CPD/120235/peerguide.pdf (accessed May 2007).

General Teaching Council for England (2006b) *The Annual Report*. London: GTCE.

General Teaching Council for Northern Ireland (2007) *Teaching: the Reflective Profession*. Belfast: GTCNI.

General Teaching Council for Scotland (2006) *The Standard for Full Registration*. Edinburgh: GTCS.

Guskey, T. (2002) 'Does it make a difference? Evaluating professional development'. *Educational Leadership*, 59(6): 45–51.

Haddon, M. (2003) *The Curious Incident of the Dog in the Night-Time*. London: Jonathan Cape.

Health and Safety Executive (2003) *Managing Work-Related Stress: A Guide for Managers and Teachers in Schools*. London: HSE.

Honey, P. and Mumford, A. (2006) *The Learning Styles Questionnaire*. Maidenhead: Peter Honey Publications.

Malderez, A. and Bodoczky, C. (1999) *Mentor Courses – A Resource Book for Trainers*. Cambridge: Cambridge University Press.

Martin, J. and Holt, A. (2002) *Joined Up Governance*. Ely: Adamson Books.

National Foundation for Educational Research (2004) *Survey of Teachers 2004: Final Report*. http://www.gtce.org.uk/research/tsurvey/2004survey/ (accessed May 2007).

Portner, H. (2002) *Mentoring New Teachers*. Thousand Oaks, CA: Corwin Press.

Richards, C. (2000) 'You don't have to be a genius but ...' [Letter]. *Times Educational Supplement*, 7 January.

Thewlis, M. (2006) *The Induction and Training and Development Experiences of Newly-Qualified Teachers and Teachers in the Second and Third Year of their Careers*. London: TDA.

Totterdell, M., Heilbronn, R., Bubb, S. and Jones, C. (2002) *Evaluation of the Effectiveness of the Statutory Arrangements for the Induction of Newly Qualified Teachers*, Research Report no. 338. Nottingham: DfES.

Training and Development Agency for Schools (2007a) *Career Entry and Development Profile 2007/8*. London: TDA. http://www.tda.gov.uk/upload/resources/pdf/c/careeranddevlopment profile2007_08.pdf (accessed May 2007).

Training and Development Agency for Schools (2007b) *The Framework of Professional Standards for Teachers*. London: TDA.

Training and Development Agency for Schools (2007c) *Continuing Professional Development: A Strategy for Teachers*. London: TDA.

*I*NDEX

Index

Key: <u>Definitive reference</u>
      Significant reference
      Other reference